LUCY BALDWIN AND LAURA ABBOTT

PREGNANCY AND NEW MOTHERHOOD IN PRISON

POLICY PRESS SHORTS RESEARCH

First published in Great Britain in 2024 by

Policy Press, an imprint of
Bristol University Press
University of Bristol
1–9 Old Park Hill
Bristol
BS2 8BB
UK
t: +44 (0)117 374 6645
e: bup-info@bristol.ac.uk

Details of international sales and distribution partners are available at
policy.bristoluniversitypress.co.uk

© Bristol University Press 2024

British Library Cataloguing in Publication Data
A catalogue record for this book is available from the British Library

ISBN 978-1-4473-6338-5 hardcover
ISBN 978-1-4473-6339-2 ePub
ISBN 978-1-4473-6340-8 ePdf

The right of Lucy Baldwin and Laura Abbott to be identified as authors of this work has
been asserted by them in accordance with the Copyright, Designs and Patents Act 1988.

Cover design: Bristol University Press
Front cover image: shutterstock/baldyrgan
Bristol University Press and Policy Press use environmentally
responsible print partners.
Printed and bound in Great Britain by CPI Group (UK) Ltd,
Croydon, CR0 4YY

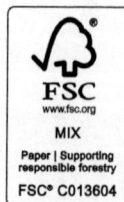

FSC
www.fsc.org
MIX
Paper | Supporting
responsible forestry
FSC® C013604

This book contains painful testimonies of experiences of pregnancy and birth that may be triggering for some.

If you are affected, support can be found with the Birth Trauma Association (www.birthtraumaassociation.org.uk).

This book is dedicated to Aisha Cleary (aka Baby A), and to Brooke-Leigh Powell (aka Baby B), two babies who were born and died in prison, and in tragic and, most significantly, *avoidable* circumstances. We must never allow it to happen again.

Likewise, to the baby stillborn in an ambulance between prison and hospital, for whom there was no inquiry.

Also to Michelle, Beth and Emma, three mums who lost their babies to local authority care. Following the forced separation from their babies, the impact was such for Michelle, Beth and Emma that they went into a 'downward spiral'. Subsequently, all three mothers went on to lose their own lives.

We remember you all here and give our promise to keep fighting for better.

Contents

Acknowledgements

We would like to wholeheartedly thank all of the mothers who have contributed to our research. We remain the conduits for your voice and will assist you to be heard. We feel humbled by your bravery, impassioned by your experiences, and are angry alongside you. Together we are stronger.

We would especially like to thank Louise and Paige, and Michelle and Sam, for their invaluable contributions to the book and to our thinking, but more than that, for their bravery and willingness to share their experiences to try to ensure no other mothers go through what they did. We hear you; we are with you.

Finally, we would like to thank Bristol University Press for their patience and for their willingness to publish this important book, the first in the UK on pregnancy, new motherhood and prison. It was a trying and long process, but we got there in the end, and we hope it will be very much worth the wait (much like a pregnancy!).

ONE

Context and landscape of pregnancy and new motherhood in prison

'My Brooke was beautiful, my daughter should be here now, I was let down, and my daughter was let down by the people who were meant to look after us.'

Louise Powell, 2022[1]

Introduction

This introductory chapter will open the conversation around pregnancy and new motherhood in prison. Having provided the context and explored the mother and baby unit (MBU) application process, the chapter will bring to the fore some of the tragic losses that have underpinned the drive for improvement in the care of pregnant and new mothers in prison. The chapter will then highlight our underpinning research and will make clear our position as researchers and practitioners.

In March 2019 both authors, together with women who have lived experience, other academics and practitioners, including from the Royal College of Midwives and the charities Birth Companions[2] and Children Heard and Seen, gave televised evidence to the Joint Human Rights Committee (JHRC).[3] Despite the lifelong implications of separation, or the trauma of being pregnant in prison, until recently very little was known about the experiences of women in such circumstances, particularly women from ethnic minority backgrounds. Pregnancy and imprisonment is a topic that has recently begun garnering interest. The subject had previously not enjoyed a particularly high profile, politically, academically or in terms of public interest. However, in more recent times the excellent work and campaigning of charities like Birth Companions and Women in Prison,[4] and important publications of the authors and others (Raikes and Lockwood, 2011; Galloway et al, 2014; O'Keefe and Dixon, 2015; Baldwin and Epstein, 2017; Dolan et al, 2019; Minson, 2020; Baldwin, 2022a, 2022b; Epstein et al, 2022), has shone light on the experiences of imprisoned mothers and babies. Consequently, the experiences and needs of this previously largely invisible population are now being discussed and, importantly, being considered in prison policy development and practice. Significantly, with a view to effecting meaningful change for the first time in many decades, not least via the Ministry of Justice's *Review of Operational Policy on Pregnancy, Mother and Baby Units and Maternal Separation* published in July 2022.[5]

Currently, it is estimated that 600 pregnant women are held in prisons in England and Wales and that some 100 babies are born to women in prison every year (Cahalin et al, 2021), however, this is an estimate only as, until very recently, data around pregnancy, miscarriage and births in prison were not formally collated. There are 12 female prisons in England, of which six have MBUs, where mothers can be housed with their babies up to 18 months old (exceptionally this can be extended to two years). Most women are offered a routine pregnancy test on reception into prison and subsequently many women only find out they are pregnant at this point of entering prison. However, as the tragic death of Brooke-Leigh Powell (Baby B) shows, this is not a failproof system.

MBUs are separate (but also within) the main prison, with individual rooms and some flexibility and deviation from the normal prison regime. Imprisoned or soon-to-be-imprisoned mothers with eligible aged children (0–18 months) and expectant mothers can apply for a place.[6] A multi-agency board assesses the application and makes and delivers the decision to the mother. The applications should ideally occur before mothers come into prison (if eligible), or as soon as possible after reception, however places are not guaranteed. Mothers who are unsuccessful or who do not apply for a space will be separated from their babies shortly after the birth and returned to prison.

Mother and baby unit applications

Sikand (2015), in her study of MBU applications, found that in the UK under-occupancy of MBUs has been an issue because the rejection rate is high. Though there is some inconsistency among units, with some MBUs being consistently fuller than others. This inconsistency warranted reflection on the manner in which boards are appointed and how decisions are being made. Sikand (2015) found that the single most important factor in the rejection/refusal of MBU applications was the social work assessment. However, importantly, in not all circumstances had the social worker undertaking the assessment either physically met the mother and baby, physically been to a MBU or sometimes both. In her report titled 'Applications to mother and baby units in prison: How decisions are made and the role of social work: A case review of social work decision making', Trowler (Chief Social Worker for Children and Families) raised some significant issues and made important recommendations for practice (Trowler, 2022). The investigation was restricted to the MBU admission decision-making process in the immediate months preceding the review. The core aim of the project was to examine the local authority social work contribution to the MBU board, but there were additional and significant issues raised during this review that merited further consideration. Particularly given that the broader goal of the review was to improve the experiences of babies and children with mothers in prison and the mothers themselves.

The report found that out of the 39 MBU applications reviewed, the panel agreed that both the decision and the decision-making process by the board was reasonable in 25 of the cases (this equates to 64 per cent). The report further stated that '[a] number of these cases showed examples of good practice and engagement by social workers and the Board members. These included high quality evidence provided by social workers which demonstrated a clear understanding of the functions of an MBU and full and cohesive multidisciplinary approaches' (Trowler, 2022: 7). However, the review panel also found that there was cause for concern in 14 of the 39 rejected applications (36 per cent). In three cases the panel felt that the decision made was 'not reasonable'. In other cases, the panel found that there was a lack of social worker involvement in 10 of the 39 rejected applications, with social workers either not attending the MBU board hearing, not writing a report for the MBU board hearing, or both. Furthermore, where there *was* social worker engagement, this was deemed below standard in three of the 39 rejected applications. It goes without saying that the impact of a forced separation on both mother and baby at this crucial stage is often profound and long-lasting (O'Malley et al, 2021). Significantly, and in line with the authors' research findings, the review panel found a lack of support for women throughout the MBU application process and a lack of scrutiny of the MBU boards' decisions.

Trowler's (2022) review of social work involvement in MBU applications also found that in 36 per cent of the rejected applications there was 'cause for concern', meaning that in 64 per cent of cases Trowler felt that the correct decision had been made. Significantly, in the rejected applications Trowler found the social work involvement lacking and, echoing Sikand (2015), found that in those instances the social workers had often not met the mothers or been inside a prison MBU.

Trowler's recommendations (among others) include improved advocacy and emotional support for pregnant women, new mothers and separating mothers, timely applications and boards being supported, monitoring and accountability in relation to decision outcomes, and local social work MBU advisers. Furthermore, in recognition of the relative powerlessness of the mother in the application process, Trowler suggested that the 'Ministry of Justice and HM Prison and Probation Service (HMPPS) should explore whether providing legal representation to mothers as part of the application process would improve outcomes for women and their children' (Trowler, 2022: 8).

Trowler goes on to say: 'I now look forward to working with partners across government, the prison estate and the third sector to take forward the recommendations from this Review and ensure that our MBU application process is making the right decisions for women and children' (Trowler, 2022: 6). It feels important to state that this book was written during a time in which there have been positive policy developments, and the intention is that more will follow, but it is also important to note that these developments followed in the wake of several very tragic events.

As already mentioned, the collective evidence provided to the JHRC in 2019 highlighted the inconsistency of care and the associated risks surrounding pregnancy in prison, the impact on families and children, and the toll all of this takes on the mothers themselves.[7] For example:

We would also like to alert the Committee to dangerous practices in prisons where women are denied access to qualified maternity practitioners when in labour. This risks the health of mother and newborn and risks a breach of Article 2. If a woman is denied access to maternity care

which results in harm, we argue this could be a breach
of Article 3. (JHRC, 2019)

We emphasised to the JHRC the potential risks surrounding
cell births, and tragically our worst fears were to come to
fruition only six months later with the death of Aisha Cleary
(Baby A), born to a mother in her cell and, unbelievably,
repeated less than two years later with the death of Brooke-
Leigh Powell (Baby B), born in her mother's cell toilet.
Obviously, investigations followed, and the care of both
mothers was unsurprisingly found lacking.

Thus, since 2018, two precious babies have been born dead
to mothers who had given birth in their cells, and another baby
was stillborn after the mother gave birth in an ambulance on
the way to hospital. As we, and the mothers' voices herein, will
highlight, pregnancy and new motherhood in prison can be a
challenging and difficult experience. For some mothers and/or
their babies it has proved a dangerous and/or fatal experience.

O'Malley and Baldwin (2019) shared the narrative of a woman
residing in a Northern Irish prison (Roseanne), who died by
suicide soon after learning she would be separated from her
baby. Similarly, in England, Michelle Barnes, a pregnant mother
in prison, was forcibly separated from her newborn baby and
returned to prison, only to take her own life five days later. Ms
A and Ms B (aka Louise Powell) tragically both gave birth to
stillborn babies in prison, one in a cell overnight and alone, the
other in a cell toilet. The mothers' experiences are briefly detailed
in the following section. The awful experiences of these mothers
painfully highlight both the psychological harm forced separations
can cause and the dangers of imprisoning pregnant mothers.

Experiences of mothers: the danger of unsupported separations

Michelle Barnes

During the period of both authors' research, a tragic death
by suicide of a mother of three, who had been incarcerated

for drugs offences, occurred. Michelle Barnes had complex needs and several risk factors. Michelle was in prison for the first time and had a history of substance abuse and impulsive self-harming behaviour. She was living with serious mental health problems which increased her risk of postnatal mental illness. Social services had just been granted an interim care order for her other children and she had been pre-warned that her new baby was likely to be placed into foster care and adopted. An Assessment, Care in Custody and Teamwork (ACCT) had been opened on Michelle in prison in the September because of concerns about her mental wellbeing and her distress at the impending removal of her baby at birth.[8] Michelle had given birth by caesarean section on 11 December 2015. Social services were granted an interim care order on the same day.

From the Prisons and Probation Ombudsman report

On 13 December, Ms Barnes was discharged from hospital. She was taken back to the hospital to feed her baby on 14 December but the next day, prison managers decided to stop these visits, without any explanation or discussion with Ms Barnes or the relevant agencies. On the evening of 16 December, Ms Barnes had appeared upset. At 11.00pm, an officer checked to see if she was more settled but got no response and could not see her. He called the night manager who went into the cell and found Ms Barnes had hanged herself. Staff began cardiopulmonary resuscitation and called an ambulance. Paramedics arrived and took over emergency treatment but shortly afterwards, recorded that Ms Barnes had died. (PPO, 2016: 1)

The subsequent Prisons and Probation Ombudsman's (PPO) report found a number of failings in the care of Michelle Barnes at HMP Low Newton. The PPO found that the root cause was the failure to plan for the postnatal period and a chaotic, ad hoc response to an already vulnerable, but now additionally traumatised, mother. There was a lack of a central figure responsible for overseeing Ms Barnes' care, resulting in a fragmented approach. The absence of a multidisciplinary meeting prevented a comprehensive discussion on her pregnancy and postnatal care. A coordinated care plan involving a midwife, mental health nurse, substance misuse keyworker, general practitioner (GP) and offender supervisor was not developed. Collaboration between community midwives and the mental health team was absent. Additionally, no separation plan was established to support Ms Barnes while the local authority took custody of her baby.

There was little recognition of the particular issues for women in Low Newton's safer custody policy, with no mention of pregnancy, separation from children or postnatal depression. The lack of multidisciplinary planning meant that decisions about Ms Barnes' postnatal care were taken on an ad hoc basis. There was poor communication within the prison and with Ms Barnes, and little coordination between the different agencies. None of the professionals who had been closely involved with Ms Barnes were booked to see her after she returned from hospital. She had no postnatal review of her medication and no mental health assessment. Although the offender supervisor originally told the social worker that Ms Barnes would not be taken back to the hospital after the birth, prison managers then made a well-intentioned, ad hoc decision to allow Ms Barnes to visit and feed her baby twice daily. However, visitation was then abruptly ended and the reasons for this were not clearly or empathically relayed to Ms Barnes. The subsequent abrupt cancellation of breastfeeding (there was no consideration for the suddenness of cessation of breastfeeding and the physiological reaction this would have caused) and a lack of necessary support increased her risk of harm, but this was not registered. After much miscommunication and change Ms Barnes was told by an officer she did not know, and who was somewhat confused in their delivery, that contact was ceased. It was not made clear to Ms Barnes that this was a prison manager decision at that time and not the final court decision.

Ms Barnes died a violent death by hanging and the PPO investigation highlighted the flaws in her care, stating:

> Her (post-natal) care was uncoordinated and ad hoc. None of the professionals who had previously been involved checked her and a decision to allow her to visit and feed her baby in hospital was suddenly reversed without proper consideration or explanation. Communication between prison staff and other agencies was poor. To compound matters, Ms Barnes' risk of suicide was not managed well – staff unaccountably decided to end suicide and self-harm monitoring before the birth, even though Ms Barnes' distress about the imminent removal of her baby had been identified as a trigger for potential suicide. No one identified the postnatal risk, and an opportunity to begin monitoring again was missed at a post-closure review. (PPO, 2016)

Following the investigation into Ms Barnes' death and recommendations from the PPO report, His Majesty's Prison (HMP) Low Newton implemented a number of important changes. Among these changes are an allocated perinatal offender manager, cross-agency training between HMP and obstetric and safeguarding teams, advocacy for perinatal mothers, continued consistent maternity caseload management and greater access to midwives within the HMP environment. Further improvements (among others) included the development of a Maternity Care Pathway (in line with the Birth Companions Birth Charter of 2016) and the development of a new role, Specialist Midwife for Vulnerable Women, in the judicial system. The HMP Low Newton model of perinatal care is regarded as best practice and will hopefully be rolled out across the whole of the female estate.

Michelle is not the only tragedy to occur in the prison estate in recent years. The tragic loss of three stillborn babies, two born in prison and one en route to hospital, further painfully highlight the potential harm of incarcerated pregnancies.

The dangers of an incarcerated pregnancy

Miranda Davies, a senior fellow at the independent health think tank the Nuffield Trust, reported that pregnant women in prison faced significant risks. Their analysis showed that in 2017–2018 roughly one in ten pregnant women gave birth either in their prison cell or en route to hospital, raising questions about their ability to access the right care.[9]

Ms A

Ms A was an 18-year-old care leaver who was remanded to prison, her first time in prison. On 27 September 2019, Ms A gave birth to a baby in her cell overnight. Ms A had found out she was pregnant while in police custody in February 2019. During her imprisonment the PPO stated that Ms A had not fully engaged with social services or her antenatal care (having at various times stated she was no longer pregnant). She was aware that social services were likely to take her baby into care at birth and as such was 'sad, angry and scared'.[10] There was some confusion about Ms A's due date because she would not agree to be scanned and she was 'small for dates'. Ms A had been labelled by some as being 'difficult'. Although according to Taylor (2021), Ms A, appeared to have been regarded as difficult and having a 'bad attitude' rather than as a vulnerable 18-year-old, who found it difficult to trust professionals and who was frightened that her baby would be taken away. There were repeated unsuccessful attempts made to engage Ms A with multiple agencies both in and out of prison during her pregnancy.

From the Prisons and Probation Ombudsman's report

The PPO investigation into the death of the baby in HMP Bronzefield found that 'Ms A' had experienced a dragging pain similar to period pain on the day of the birth. Ms A said she had pressed her bell and asked for a nurse and the officer asked her why she needed one. She told him that she needed help and a nurse and an ambulance. Ms A stated she rang her cell bell later when no nurse came but got no reply and 'gave up asking for help' after that. Ms A said that she was on all fours when a torch was shone into her cell. By about 11pm, she was in constant pain and could not get to the cell bell to ring for help. She said she lost consciousness because of the pain and when she came around, her baby was there. Ms A managed to bite through the umbilical cord and tie it in a knot. She put the placenta on the floor and wrapped the baby in a towel. She said her baby was purple and not breathing. There was blood on the floor, and she tried to wipe it up but more came out of her. She put the placenta in the waste bin and got back into bed with her baby (PPO, 2021: 19). Ms A spent the rest of the night in her cell alone with her apparently dead baby. Fellow prisoners alerted staff to Ms A and prison staff eventually came into the cell and instigated emergency procedures. On-call nursing staff attended to Ms A and attempted rescue breaths and use of oxygen on the baby, however no infant equipment was available and so a seal couldn't be obtained. Paramedics arrived at the scene approximately 30 minutes after Ms A's cell was opened and they confirmed the baby was not alive. Ms A and her baby were taken to hospital by ambulance. The pathologist was unable to determine definitively whether Baby A was born alive or was stillborn. The pathologist gave the cause of death as ante/intra-partum hypoxia/ischaemia (a lack of oxygen to the brain either before or during birth) due to delayed chorionic villous maturation and a single umbilical artery (PPO, 2021: 23:143).[11] The PPO report identified a number of multi-agency failings in the care of Ms A, stating that Ms A gave birth alone in her cell overnight without medical assistance. This should never have happened. Overall, the healthcare offered to Ms A was not equivalent to that she could have expected in the community (PPO, 2021). Sadly, Ms A's case was not an isolated incident and only nine months after the death of Baby A, another baby, a girl, was stillborn at HMP Styal.

Ms B (aka Louise Powell) and baby Brooke-Leigh Powell

Ms B, Louise Powell, was sentenced to her first prison sentence of 35 weeks in prison in March 2020. Louise had been offered the routine pregnancy test on her reception into prison but had refused the test, believing it was "impossible" for her to be pregnant because she did "not have sexual relationships with men". Over the next few months no one, Louise included, had any reason to suspect she was pregnant. Louise is a very slim woman but did not 'show'. Not even her cell mate, an experienced mother, had thought she looked in any way pregnant. However, it transpired that Louise had been raped. Louise believes someone had sex with her without her consent while she was under the influence of alcohol (or that she may have been 'spiked'). Louise has no memory of the event at all, thus, as far as she was concerned, it was impossible for her to be pregnant as she had not had sex with a man (Louise identifies as gay). On 18 June 2020, Louise Powell gave birth to her daughter, Brooke-Leigh Powell, in her cell toilet at HMP Styal. Louise firmly believes that "because of the prison system's failures and lack of care", she "was robbed not just of a positive birth experience" but also of her "right to be the mother of baby Brooke", who Louise will "always believe died during her birth", and after help was unacceptably delayed.

From the Prisons and Probation Ombudsman's report

On 18 June 2020, just after lunchtime, Louise began to bleed and feel pain. Believing she was having a period she didn't think much of it. The pain increased over time and at this point her cell mate suggested Louise was in labour. Louise was still adamant at this point that this was not possible. Over the next few hours Louise's pain increased and she asked for pain relief. However, the nurse mistakenly stated that she had given Louise paracetamol earlier in the day (she had not) and so refused to attend and see Louise. The senior officer (SO) on duty noted that Louise's stomach was swollen, remarking that she 'looked six months pregnant', and again asked if Louise could be pregnant, Louise said no, but did state that she hadn't had a period since November 2019. The SO rang the nurse again, who again declined to attend to Louise, stating that she would make her a triage appointment for the following day. An hour later the SO contacted the nurse again asking the nurse to visit because 'Ms B was getting worse. The nurse said she was just about to end her shift. She handed over to the night duty nurse that Ms B was having a painful period and might ring for paracetamol during the night' (PPO, 2022: 1:9). At HMP Styal, women are housed on 'houseblocks' which are like individual houses set in grounds. The women are locked in at night, but officers do not remain on the houseblock. Around half an hour after the previous call to healthcare, a night patrol officer spoke to Louise, who was by now in considerable pain. The officer again asked Louise if she could be pregnant, Louise again said no but asked for an ambulance as she felt something was 'very wrong'. The officer told the SO that she thought Louise needed to be seen by a nurse. The SO was about to end her shift. Before leaving the prison, she told the night orderly officer that she had contacted healthcare about Louise three times, but they had not been to see her. Louise states that her cell mate (Ms X in the report) had spoken to staff and insisted that Louise was in labour despite what Louise herself was saying, stating that she, as a mother who had experienced labour multiple times, was sure that was what was 'wrong' with Louise. Approximately 30 minutes after the patrol officer's visit the cell mate pressed the emergency bell, as:

Ms B was in so much pain. Two officers responded almost immediately. Ms B was on all fours, and they thought she appeared to be in labour, although Ms B said that was not possible as she did not have sex with men. One of the officers accompanied Ms B to the toilet. At 9.06pm, she rang the duty nurse, who arrived within 30 seconds. While the nurse was talking to Ms B, she began to give birth sitting on the toilet. The nurse radioed for an ambulance at 9.10pm, but the prison's radio system had failed a few minutes earlier and, although staff with radios could hear each other, the communications officer in the control room could not hear them. (PPO, 2022: 2:11)

Baby Brooke-Leigh, who was in the breech position, was delivered by the nurse and 'showing no signs of life'. No attempt at rescue breaths were given. A GP arrived and stated that the baby was dead. Staff wrapped baby Brooke in a blanket. Due to failures in the communication systems in the prison it was another half an hour before paramedics and an ambulance arrived. Paramedics asked what life-saving techniques had been attempted, and when they were told none, they asked: 'You have not done anything at all?' (PPO, 2022: 15:103). They then took the baby from the officer and attempted CPR on Brooke. Baby Brooke was declared dead at the scene. At 10.15pm Louise and her baby were transferred to hospital. The consultant obstetrician said that although it was not possible to be '100% sure' it appeared that baby Brooke would have been alive at the onset of labour. Louise firmly believes this to be the case as in hindsight she states that "I remember her moving, I just didn't know what that feeling was, but now I know it was her moving." Although classed as premature (at approximately 31 weeks), Brooke was a good weight and appeared as if she would in all likelihood have been a healthy baby if she had survived her birth. The PPO report stated:

The consultant obstetrician said that if Ms B had been taken to hospital by 7.30 or 8.00pm, they would have done an ultrasound scan and identified that the baby was in the breech position and would have been able to provide expert help with the delivery. She said that assuming the baby was alive during labour, the outcome 'would have been different' if Ms B had been in hospital. She added that she could not say that the baby would have been born in perfect condition, but she could say that, if the baby had been fine in labour and was stillborn because of the birth itself, they 'could have helped'. (PPO, 2022: 16:114)

Louise was returned to the prison at around 5.30am, as although the hospital had wanted to admit her, she wanted to be "back with her friends for support". The PPO report states that 'Ms B provided us with a detailed statement of her post-natal care at Styal'. Ms B said she received good care after the death of Baby B but she felt that this was too late and she should have been taken to hospital earlier in the evening of 18 June. Louise herself has stated that it is her view that had she been sent to hospital, she would have been given a caesarean section and her daughter would be alive. She said the prison had reassured her that measures had been taken to ensure continuity of care with her community GP after her release but that this 'had not happened' (PPO, 2022: 16:109). Louise Powell's solicitor, Jane Ryan of Bhatt Murphy, said: 'There were multiple missed opportunities to help Louise. There was no system in place to recognise unexpected birth at the time. It is inhumane to leave a woman howling in pain unaided and forced to give birth in a toilet.'[12] The legal case is ongoing. Brooke-Leigh Powell would have been three years old on 18 June 2023.

The PPO reports into the deaths of babies 'A and B' (published in September 2021 and January 2022 respectively), state that neither event 'should have happened', that 'serious error of judgement' occurred, and that delays and inadequacies in healthcare provision, alongside delays in accessing emergency medical intervention, contributed to the deaths of the babies. The PPO states that it considers 'that all pregnancies in prison should be treated as high risk by virtue of the fact that the woman is locked behind a door for a significant amount of time' (PPO, 2021: 3:28). This led the PPO to conclude that for effective and importantly safe oversight of pregnant women in prison to occur, it is required that (PPO, 2021):

- there is a clear perinatal pathway;
- the midwifery service is integrated with healthcare;
- healthcare staff have clinical expertise with pregnant women;
- the midwifery service is tailored to the specific needs of pregnant women in a custodial setting; and
- care is able to take account of women who do not want to engage with maternity and healthcare services.

The PPO reports (2021, 2022) echoed previous recommendations, and although they described unexpected births in prison as 'rare', added that there was a need for national guidance to be provided to staff concerning what to do in the event of an unexpected birth. Specifically stating:

> We recommend: The Head of HMPPS Women's Team, in conjunction with NHS England, should provide guidance for all staff in women's prisons on what to do in the event of an unexpected birth. This should emphasise the need to obtain a rapid response from the ambulance service to guide staff through rescue breaths and keeping the baby warm. (PPO, 2022: 23:150)

Furthermore, in recognition that prison nurses are usually not registered midwives, and that in the UK it is a legal violation for anyone other than a registered midwife or medical practitioner to attend women in childbirth (except in 'sudden or urgent necessity', Nursing and Midwifery Order, 2001), the PPO recommended that prison healthcare staff, and specifically nurses, should all receive additional training in recognising the signs of early labour with a view to ensuring imprisoned labouring women are taken to hospital in a timely manner.

There has never been an inquiry into the death of the baby born dead in ambulance en route from HMP Bronzefield to the hospital in 2017, so there is scant information about that mother or her baby's circumstances, meaning we are unable to comment on any 'lessons learned' from this occurrence or the circumstances surrounding this stillbirth. Nonetheless, the mother and her baby are acknowledged and remembered here.

These mothers' experiences are a tragic reminder of why we, the authors, do what we do, and why as activist researchers we continue to challenge the system to be safer and different. Although in most cases a community order is likely to be more appropriate, there is no doubt that for some imprisoned women, MBUs provide a safe space and opportunity for a mother to remain with her baby. Indeed, in some cases mothers might otherwise have lost custodial care of their babies, and the MBU provides the opportunity of a supported beginning that will enable a mother to remain with her child post-release. There is no doubt that good work goes on in an MBU, and some staff are dedicated to supporting mothers and their babies to stay together. However, do such supportive and wonderful environments need to exist within a prison? We argue not, but also that while they do, mothers and babies should have the best care possible, and part of that best care comes from learning from the past and understanding what is needed in the future. Which is where our research comes in. Our calls for change are evidence- and practice-based, and passion-driven, and our own research underpins our discissions and positionality.

The authors' underpinning research

Baldwin's study, 'Motherhood challenged', is the largest on motherhood and the experience of prison in the UK to date. It explored the impact of imprisonment on mothers and grandmothers (57 mothers in total contributed to the study). The study, although not exclusively involving pregnant and new mothers, offered insight and recommendations concerning those experiences and, importantly, also on motherhood experiences more generally. Forty-three mothers from England and Wales contributed to the study via qualitative interviews (28) and letter correspondence (25 letters from 15 mothers). The research was feminist and qualitative in design and method. Qualitative research approaches facilitate the feminist exploration of lived experiences, the meanings, emotions, feelings and thoughts (Bryman and Burgess, 2002; Renzetti, 2013). A qualitative research orientation regarding method and research tools was adopted from the outset, thus valuing the exploration of individual experiences, individuals themselves, their responses to and perceptions of their position and lived experience. Interviews and letters were analysed thematically.

Baldwin did not specifically ask the mothers about their offence, although most mothers in the study chose to disclose something. All bar two disclosed offences that were nonviolent in nature. From what was known (that is, disclosed), the mothers could be crudely categorised into one of three main categories: mothers who had issues with addiction and had offended to fund their habit (or the habits of others); mothers in poverty who stated they had offended to provide/survive; and mothers who had made a 'one off' mistake of varying gravity. Most of the mothers in the study disclosed traumatic histories typical of women who experience prison (Corston, 2007), importantly, all of the mothers also demonstrated strength and resilience and were emphatic that they had 'survived' prison. All of the mothers were involved in or had access to their children prior to custody, either via shared care, visitation or as a primary carer. Most children were cared for by grandmothers, and six mothers in the study lost the care of their children either permanently or temporarily to their local authority as a direct result of their sentence (three were eventually returned to at least partial maternal care). Eight mothers in the study were pregnant when sentenced, although not all knew this (reiterating the importance of reception pregnancy testing and a later offer to test if refused). Several mothers in the study had children outside or in care who were of an age that would have made them eligible to apply for MBU spaces. None of those with eligible children outside chose to make an MBU application. The study revealed new information about the lack of care and support afforded to mothers and grandmothers, before, during and long after prison. It evidenced the sometimes devastating, sometimes fatal, impact on mothers (and their children) when maternal needs and maternal trauma was not accommodated or responded to. Furthermore, the study highlighted the relationship between motherhood and desistance by demonstrating how failure to support mothers struggling to mother in a range of complex circumstances or trying to renegotiate their role in the family post-release or coming to terms with children being removed from their care could be directly related to offending/desistance and rehabilitation.

Abbott's study, *The Incarcerated Pregnancy* (2018), was undertaken across three female prison estates in England. The study took place during 2015–2016 and involved semi-structured interviews with 28 female prisoners in England who were pregnant, or had recently given birth while imprisoned, ten members of staff, and ten months of non-participant observation. Follow-up interviews with five women were undertaken as their pregnancies progressed to birth and the postnatal phase. This qualitative study utilised an ethnographic approach in order to gain a rounded perspective of pregnancy experiences in prison. Using a sociological framework of Sykes' (2007 [1958]) 'pains of imprisonment', the research built upon existing knowledge, highlighting the institutional responses to the pregnant prisoner.

Conclusions demonstrated the fact that pregnancy is an anomaly within the patriarchal prison system. The main findings of the study included 'institutional thoughtlessness' (Crawley, 2005), whereby prison life continues with little thought for those with unique physical needs, such as pregnant women; and 'institutional ignominy' where the women experience shaming as a result of institutional practices which entail their being displayed in public and characterised with institutional emblems of imprisonment, such as handcuffs (Abbott et al, 2020). The study also revealed new information about coping strategies adopted by pregnant prisoners; and clarified how the women negotiated entitlements and sought information about their rights, highlighting gaps in policy guidelines. The research illuminated voices of the women and clarified their experiences, from the indignity and fear of birthing in a cell, the shame of feeling paraded in public, to the missed opportunities for change and the turning points in behaviour for some. The fieldwork provided a societal documentary, with Abbott reporting on how the environment of prison life juxtaposed the experiences of the pregnant women. Throughout the study, women described their struggles as they balanced managing their pregnancy symptoms with maintaining a sense of boldness, trying to meet their physical needs while attempting to merge into the background. The tensions of the environment created a sense of stress throughout pregnancy, potentially impacting upon a woman's physical health and that of her unborn baby. At the time of undertaking the research, guidance for pregnant women was hard to find and staff were often unaware of what women were entitled to. Women too were unaware of their rights and entitlements, and this led to disempowerment with a potential for countless consequences for the woman. At worst, this preceded distortion of the midwifery role, breaking statutory directives and rendering the pregnant woman and unborn baby susceptible to unsuitable assessment and care. The scope for impact from Abbott's work has been substantial. Abbott's hopes for the future are that we can reform the landscape for pregnant women in prison so that negative experiences detailed are not replicated and the opportunities for change are realised to their full potential.

The voices of mothers

The voices of mothers through the narratives, excerpts and biographies in this book were so important to the authors to include, not least because '[w]omen's voices and experiences are often silenced or marginalised in debates about the CJS, with little attention paid to the perspectives of women caught up in that system as suspects, defendants, prisoners and victims' (Grace et al, 2022: 2). Thus, the authors *and* the women's voices in this book make a powerful case that the inequality and injustice that surrounds criminalised women must be addressed and rectified. The mothers' experiences described herein add weight to the argument for an alternative to custody as an appropriate disposal in most cases for pregnant and new mothers facing sentence (in fact, for most women). We hope that this text will shine a light on this unique and specific criminal justice experience, and that it will, with the women's voices, be useful to interested researchers, policy makers and practitioners. However, we do not simply want this book to reach our 'interested' audience, to preach to the already converted so to speak. Instead, we would especially hope that the book could be shared with the less interested, to alert those to the significance and need for positive change in the hope that it can replace disinterest, ignorance or inaction with resolve, motivation and a passion for change – for the benefit of wider society, of course, but especially and specifically for mothers and their babies.

Each of the chapters, like *Mothering Justice* (Baldwin, 2015) before it, is interspersed with 'Pauses for thought'. These pauses ask the readers to think wider than the chapters were able to reach with their limited wordcounts, but also to encourage thought and prompt discussion (educators can use the pauses for thought as the basis of a seminar).

Conclusion

We, the authors and editors of this book, are in many ways sad that it needs to be written at all. We begin the discussion here with a clear statement of our position. We believe that in all but the most serious of cases, pregnant women should not be sentenced to imprisonment, and that community-based alternatives to prison MBUs should be actively pursued and developed. Our preference would be that no baby should or would ever have to reside with its mother in a prison space. We do not feel that prison is an appropriate or safe place for pregnant women, and we feel that community-based alternatives to the imprisonment of pregnant mothers is not only preferable, but vital to pursue as a goal. However, and that said, while we are some way away from this being a realistic option there remains a need for this book. The book will shine a reflective and critical light on the experience of pregnancy and new motherhood in the context of criminal justice. It will provide a safe space for women's voices to be heard in sharing those experiences, and it will provide knowledge, understanding and guidance for those working with pregnant and new mothers in contact with the criminal justice system (CJS).

It is imperative that policy and practice for this particularly vulnerable population must be informed by the appropriate expert practitioners and academics. Collectively our knowledge spans 70 years (35 each). Thus, this book is informed by our knowledge, evidence and practical working experience from social work and probation (Baldwin) and midwifery (Abbott). In our academic careers we have shared a passion for improving the care of all women in the CJS and our interests particularly conjoin at motherhood, specifically motherhood, criminal justice and prison. Ergo, through this book – drawing on our current and recent research and alongside the voices and experiences of the mothers – we hope to be able to inform and progress the conversation about this difficult topic, but also to provide a resource for academics and practitioners alike.

This book is dedicated to the memories of the aforementioned lost babies and Michelle. We, as activist researchers and academics, are working with others to ensure such tragedies never, ever happen again. Notwithstanding arguments (which will be revisited later) about whether the mothers should have been imprisoned while pregnant at all, Ms A (mother from Bronzefield) and Louise Powell[13] (mother from Styal), were both clearly let down by the prison and healthcare systems. As a result of the tragic events that unfolded, both mothers suffered the unimaginable and profound loss of their much-loved babies. We can't know for sure how these two mothers will feel years after the event, or how their loss has impacted on (and will continue to impact) their lives, but as mothers ourselves we can imagine that the pain of their loss is infinite. Indeed, Louise, who is in regular contact with one of the authors, and who gave her blessing and contributed to this book, tells us there is never a day and hardly a moment when she doesn't think about her daughter Brooke. As she recently said: "I miss her every day, I should be a mum now. What happened to me should not have happened … and I want to try to make sure it never happens to anyone else" (Louise Powell, 2022).[14]

TWO

How we came to be here: 100 years of criminalised motherhood

'It is barbaric what happened to me, like something out of the dark ages.'

Louise Powell, 2023

Introduction

This chapter explores a historical perspective of pregnancy and new motherhood in prison and makes comparisons of the treatment and conditions from the past 100 years to the present day. We draw upon the similarities of the environment, care needs and experiences of women from the 1900s to the 21st century and describe the findings from campaigners' reviews and research. We discuss how these campaigns and reviews of prison conditions from 100 years ago mirror the findings of our own research and that of modern-day activists and campaigners for reform.

It is perhaps accepted wisdom that modern society has long favoured the male gender, a status quo that has contributed to the positionality of women and their experiences in society. Zedner (1991) rightly argues that gendered notions of how women, especially mothers, should and, importantly, should not behave are heavily influenced by traditional feminine (and masculine) ideology. Johnstone (2019) highlights how this translated to firmly established and gendered roles becoming established, particularly with the advancement of industrialisation and capitalism. Women's role as homemaker and nurturer became an established norm, and parenting and child-raising were (and to some extent are still) deemed to be the woman's role. To understand the connection between criminalised motherhood, imprisonment, patriarchy, religion, culture and the CJS, it is essential to acknowledge the intersectionality that shapes women's experiences. Throughout history and to this day, these factors contribute significantly to the disadvantages and discrimination faced by women in the CJS. Building upon a brief historical overview, the authors will utilise their research to present a contemporary perspective. As in the rest of the book, the focus remains on amplifying women's voices as they share their lived experiences.

100 years of pregnancy and new motherhood in prison

19th- and 20th-century women in prison

Moral judgements upon the types of women imprisoned were usual in the 16th and 17th centuries (Zedner, 1991; Bosworth, 2000). Before the beginning of single-sex prisons in the 19th century, women were often left unsupervised, predominantly at night. Prostitution, and resultant pregnancies, were commonplace, especially for those exploited by male guards while inside prison (Zedner, 1991; Bosworth, 2000). Women in the late 18th and early 19th centuries would sometimes pay to have their abdomens filled with fluid to make them look pregnant. This phenomenon, called 'pleading the belly', was employed in order to avoid hanging. Women prisoners in the 19th century were in a minority compared to men, often receiving short sentences for petty crimes (Zedner, 1991; Bosworth, 2000).

In the early 20th century attention was focused on female criminality and female biology. Women, especially mothers, were seen as a major source of dishonesty and crime. Criminal mothers were seen as immoral and judged more severely than their male counterparts due to acting outside of their gender and their maternal role. Throughout history, women have often occupied a weaker position than men, not least by the fact that women were deemed the 'possession' of their fathers and then their husbands. Women were prevented by law from accessing divorce, ownership of property, access to education and equal pay. Until 1994 a man could not be charged with the rape of his wife due to common law conjugal rights, denying women safety, even in marriage. Women in the Victorian era were expected to conform to traditional ideals of femininity (for example, docile, acquiescent, compliant, chaste and maternal). By the mid-19th century middle-class notions of femininity, family and gendered roles were firmly established, and most women conformed as such. Therefore, women who strayed outside of gender norms and expectations were seen as deviant and damaging to wider society. Further, if the deviant woman was also a mother the connection between her gender and maternal role made her doubly deviant. Early records of imprisoned motherhood experiences are lacking, particularly with reference to mothers' own voices. Historical records show that mothers were occasionally allowed to keep their babies with them in prison for up to two years. However, many children born in prison tragically died during childbirth or shortly after. The majority of imprisoned mothers belonged to the working class, and due to financial difficulties faced by their families, most of their children were sent to different institutions or the workhouse. Johnstone (2019) reported that many children were adopted without their mother's knowledge or agreement. Post-release, many mothers were returned to the disorder of their pre-prison lives and often lost contact with their children. Subsequently, mothers often continued on a trail of offending, returning to prison time and time again (Baldwin and Abbott, 2021).

Prison reform and activism in the 19th and 20th centuries

Early prison reformers like John Howard, Jeremy Bentham and Elizabeth Fry were all profoundly influenced by religion and/or rehabilitation by reform. Therefore, while being committed to improving prison conditions and treating women prisoners more humanely, the combination of religious and gendered thinking influenced early penal reformers with a focus on saving lost souls and returning women to their 'feminine virtues' (Barton, 2000). British activists like Elizabeth Fry were instrumental in implementing prison reform in the 1800s, segregating prisoners by gender and advocating the employment of female wardens (Zedner, 1991; Bosworth, 2000; Sharpe et al, 2009).

When comparing the lives of Victorian criminalised mothers with contemporary mothers, the similarities of experiences and pathways into offending are alarming. Zedner (1991) observed that mothers were imprisoned for nonviolent offences. Offences were often related to poverty, mental ill-health, substance misuse and prostitution. Again, reminiscent of the present day, in the 19th and 20th centuries mothers were most often serving short custodial sentences, leaving their children and families to cope with very little state support.

Like the campaigns and activists of the modern day, there are examples of prison reformers campaigning for the improvement of imprisoned women's lives. Between the late 19th century and early 20th century, the Duchess of Bedford (Adeline Marie Russell) was involved in several campaigns aimed at the moral and occupational improvement of women's lives (Bennett, 2017). In the 1890s she regularly visited the female-only Aylesbury and, in 1900, she became the president of the National Lady Visitors' Association, visiting women in prison to help with preparations for life following imprisonment. Bennett (2017) describes how the Duchess of Bedford, described as a prison reformer and philanthropist, made several recommendations pertaining to prison pregnancy and maternity in 1919 and 1920. Russell led an enquiry into prison conditions and brought to light not only the poor accommodation but also the inadequate conditions for pregnant women and the lack of specially trained staff. An enquiry was then commissioned specifically relating to the issue of access to medical care for pregnant women. Concerns were raised over the placing of pregnant women in ordinary prison cells with little observation and limited access to emergency assistance if it was required. There were also fears about the anxiety caused by locking up and isolating women later in their pregnancies. Recommendations included pregnant women having improved access to healthcare, and staff specially trained in maternity care. The enquiry also highlighted the rights of the unborn and babies born in prison. In 1919, it was questioned by the activists, reformers and women whether babies should be born in prison at all (Baldwin and Abbott, 2021).

Reports of pregnant women giving birth in prison during the 19th century served as a catalyst for political change. Recommendations were made to provide appropriate care for pregnant women outside of jail (Mayhew and Binny, 2011). The separation of women from their babies was frequently used as a form of punishment, along with other control measures like branding, handcuffing and strapping (Garland, 1985). However, policies regarding pregnancy and motherhood were inconsistent, lacking standardised care or agreed timelines for separating mothers from their children.

Present-day reviews and reform

The recent Ministry of Justice review on the policy of pregnancy and separation, concerning children under two years old, uncovered worrying findings and raised questions similar to those addressed in the 1919 Russell review. These include issues related to the shortage of specialised staff and the presence of babies in prison. The fundamental questions that are still being asked are whether it is appropriate to accommodate pregnant women, mothers and their babies in prison at all or whether alternative community-based models such as the one practised by Jasmine Mother's Recovery[1] would be more fitting in most circumstances, principally when the nature of their mothers' offending is most often low level and low risk of harm.

The new mandatory policy driven from the Ministry of Justice review has been statutory since September 2021 (Minstry of Justice and HMPPS, 2021).[2] Meetings are held regularly to ensure the policy is being actioned on the ground with organisations such as the charity Birth Companions,[3] health professionals, HMPPS staff and both authors in attendance. Abbott recently set up the Prison Midwives Action Group (PMAG), where prison midwives from around the country meet to share experiences, good practice and whether the new policy is working at ground level. From these meetings, Abbott can share issues and challenges with the HMPPS women's team and shine a light on practices that may be problematic for pregnant women and new mothers in prison (present-day reform will be revisited in the closing chapter).

Pause for thought

- What are your thoughts about the progress (or lack of) in relation to mothers and imprisonment?
- Why do you think we have been so slow to collect/collate figures?
- What are your thoughts around babies 'in prison'?
- Are your thoughts influenced by a scenario where it would mean forced mother–child separation – *or* prison?

Evidence from Baldwin and Abbott's research and the contemporary landscape

Anxiety, stress and shame

The research undertaken by both Baldwin and Abbott with imprisoned mothers revealed that being pregnant in prison is often a humiliating, stressful and frightening experience.

Baldwin reported that mothers-to-be generally felt protective over their 'belly' and fearful of volatile situations which may lead to their baby becoming harmed: "I kept my hands on my belly all the time … it was instinct, like I was protecting her" (Kady). Similarly, Abbott found that women would often want to hide their growing pregnancy bump for fear of violence against them and wanting the pregnancy to remain hidden for as long as possible: "I wanted to hide my bump so I wore baggy tops so nobody could tell I was pregnant. You don't know who is in here, or for what crime so it was scary to think someone might want to hurt my baby" (Trixie).

Abbott's research fieldnotes describes women living with fighting and violence at times, and rising tensions in prisons, often while under 'lockdown'[4] for several days. This would cause understandable fear for pregnant women, especially in the last trimester. Women in Abbott's research were concerned about not having enough food and the impact this might have on their unborn babies. Although clear directions and policy guidance about the additional nutrition pregnant women should receive exist, staff were often ignorant, or confused by the policy, or were inconsistent with their provision. Instead of routinely, some women would get additional food in the form of 'pregnancy packs', while other weeks these packs would stop for no reason. Women across all the research (and reminiscent of Victorian times), described feeling hungry, losing weight and relying on of the kindness of individual officers and other prisoners. However, reflecting the sad reality of their often-complex needs and lives before prison, several mothers across all the studies stated that by being in prison they felt that they were 'safer' and better provided for than they might have been outside: "My life was so chaotic I wouldn't have attended any appointments or had anyone care for me outside, ironically me and my baby were safer in there [prison], at least I was warm and not being battered" (Emma). Mothers worried about their own and their baby's wellbeing alongside additional anxiety about whether or not they would secure a space on the MBU, or whether they would be separated from their newborn. Many mothers described the stress of the unknown and uncertainty if they would be separated from their child as particularly traumatic (Abbott et al, 2023a).

Imprisoned pregnant mothers worry about access to midwives and specialist healthcare and are especially fearful of labouring and giving birth alone in their cells. Abbott's research demonstrated unpredictability in the delivery of healthcare and midwifery care. Although good in places, it was often inconsistent, with no cover for when a midwife was on sick leave or on holiday (Abbott et al, 2023b). Baldwin's research resonated with these findings and women would describe their fears of being pregnant in prison, especially being alone when in labour: "I was literally terrified of going into labour at night on my own and I had nightmares about giving birth on my own, my babies come quick they do, it's a really scary place to be pregnant" (Tarian). Both Baldwin and Abbott spoke to mothers who had experienced labour and birth in their cells.

Abbott et al (2020) describe how Layla, a second-time mother, was ignored by prison staff despite repeatedly telling them she was in labour. Despite not being appropriately qualified, healthcare nurses denied that Layla was in labour, leaving her feeling terrified and powerless. Layla's baby was premature and lying in the breech position (bottom first). Her baby was born in the prison cell with no midwifery or obstetric expertise – a potentially dangerous, life-threatening situation for both mother and baby. The staff described Layla and her baby as being lucky to have been physically unscathed. However, Layla had been deeply traumatised by the situation and the mental scars of fearing for her life and that of her baby were apparent many months following the birth: "The nurses were not even trained in midwifery whatsoever … they were telling me that I wasn't in labour, so I ended up having (baby) in my cell" (Layla). Furthermore, Layla did not know if she would be permitted a space on the MBU or whether she would be separated from her baby or not, or even whether she should breastfeed her baby. The uncertainty for a new mother who had experienced a traumatic and dangerous birth only added to her pain. Mirroring previous research, our studies found that the period of waiting to hear if their application to the MBU had been successful or not was incredibly stressful. Mothers who 'knew' they would be separated from their babies at birth described their awful feelings of 'impending doom'. Mothers described feeling desperate to bond with their babies while still in utero, "in the hope somehow he will remember I loved him" (Helen).

Pregnant women in Abbott's study described 'putting off' thinking about the point of separation until they 'had to', fundamentally because it was just 'too hard'. Others described how it was *all* they thought about: "I'm anxious ... I can't sleep at night, like I need to know now, I want to know. It's my baby. I want them to tell me if I'm allowed my baby or not" (Abi). Women's stress was compounded by how late in their pregnancies decisions about their MBU place was made. In Baldwin's study, 'Kady' did not find out about her space until after her baby was born and described how this felt: "I went to hospital to give birth not knowing if I was coming back with my baby or not, I had my mum on standby ... it was awful" (Kady). This echoed findings in Abbott's study where feelings of anticipatory and disenfranchised grief together with deep uncertainty were commonplace for women (Abbott et al, 2023a). The Lost Mothers project, led by Abbott and funded by the Economic and Social Research Council, exploring how women and professionals involved with the CJS experience enforced separation of newborn babies, will further examine and subsequently shine a light on this area.[5]

Abbott's research described how pregnant women would feel that emblems of prison life such as handcuffs and prison uniforms contributed to their indignity, particularly when being escorted to hospital appointments heavily pregnant. Sammy described how she felt 'judged' and defensive when attending the hospital in handcuffs with uniformed officers.

'You've got all the mums and the dads, husbands and wives, sitting there holding their precious little bump, and there I am walking in and they just looked at me like I was filth. And it's like, I've just made a mistake, I was stupid; I haven't hurt anybody, I'm a good mum.' (Sammy)

Baldwin also evidenced the internal shame felt by the mothers: "I'm tainted now ain't I? Forever … I'll always be that mum that went to jail. Every time I hear that song 'Tainted Love' … I think that's me that is" (Kady).

Minoritised pregnant mothers

Although many of the women in our research were from an ethnic minority, we did not specifically explore aspects of the mothers' experiences as related to their ethnicity. Research is sadly lacking in relation to intersectionality, especially surrounding the experiences of mothers from ethnic minorities. Recent research into the experiences of minoritised women and mothers in prison (Bozkurt, 2022; Thomas, 2023; Bozkurt and Thomas, 2023) makes an important contribution to the field in this area. Both Bozkurt (2022) and Thomas (2023) describe how mothers in their studies felt that their race or ethnicity placed an additional layer on their experience. A layer which impacted on how they felt about themselves and their experiences, but significantly how they felt they were responded to by others. Rarely discussed specifically are foreign national mothers in prison, and mothers who are held in immigration detention centres. Although conditions for pregnant women in detention centres are 'improved', Arshad et al state:

Prior to 2016, around 100 migrant pregnant women were held each year in detention often for prolonged periods. … Since then, following a Home Office review, numbers have reduced. Women can only be detained when necessary, for up to 72 hours, but exceptionally for a week. However, it is argued that women are still being detained unnecessarily (International Detention Coalition, 2016) and that detention is harmful to their health. (Arshad et al, 2018: 2)

Pregnant asylum-seeking women are included in the 2010 National Institute for Health and Care Excellence guidelines to improve maternity services for women with complex social factors. A case series review found that pregnant migrant women in detention were seven times more likely to have a high-risk pregnancy than the average UK woman. Arshad et al (2018), in their important research into detained women's experiences, identified four key themes: 'challenges to accessing UK health care'; 'exacerbation of mental health conditions'; 'feeling hungry'; and 'lack of privacy'. They argue that their findings could be used to review maternity care in detention and ensure detention staff understand the experiences of detained pregnant women so the needs of this vulnerable group can be met. We would echo these and also suggest that when and where appropriate the recommendations contained in the aforementioned reports are extended to detention centres.

Conclusion

History repeats itself as we witness a significant number of women incarcerated for minor offences, missing out on crucial community support opportunities. Tragically, we continue to encounter cases of stillborn babies in prison cells, exposing grave failures reminiscent of the Duchess of Bedford's review. It is disheartening to realise that even after 100 years, we are still compelled to provide evidence and commentary on these tragic incidents, reflecting a Dickensian approach and attitude towards pregnant women and new mothers behind bars.

It is clear that historical practices and conditions feel closer to modern-day treatment of pregnant women and new mothers in prisons than they should. Identical issues such as health inequality, babies dying in prison cells and experiences of shame and institutional thoughtlessness persist. Activists and reformers continue to challenge, to bring light to the conditions, but like 100 years ago, change is slow. Although there are attempts being made to change the system and cross party political goodwill, the issues remain. The research evidence, the tragedies described so far, demonstrate that prison is no place for pregnant and new mothers, except in the most extreme circumstances. Over 100 years of research, audits and activism have clearly shown that the best outcomes, and best opportunities for supporting criminalised pregnant and new mothers and importantly their babies, most often lie in community settings rather than being locked away inside of prisons.

Pause for thought

- How are you feeling after reading this historical context?
- Do you see pregnancy as something that ought to be a 'mitigating circumstance' in court?
- What do you think public opinion would be about this?
- What are your immediate thoughts about your professional/academic response – what can you do?
- Reflections after reading so far?

THREE

The 'journey'
to incarcerated motherhood

'If I'd been able to get help sooner, I wouldn't have even been in there and I would still have my baby … but no one was interested until I was pregnant – we didn't stand a chance really.'

Emma Baldwin, 2015

Introduction

Reflecting on the mothers' narratives, this chapter will reveal the significance of mothers' own experiences of being mothered as well as the circumstances and context of their lives before prison. The chapter will go on to reflect on the relationship between motherhood and desistance before exploring CJS responses to criminalised mothers.

The mothers' experiences before criminalisation and/or prison: missed opportunities

For many criminalised pregnant and new mothers, the point at which they are sentenced or appear in court is often not their first foray into the CJS. Baldwin (2022b) describes a 'Circle of Circumstance' (see Figure 3.1), which is a common living space for women who will become criminalised. Most imprisoned pregnant and new mothers have experienced or are in the midst of experiencing multiple challenges, discrimination and disadvantage before they enter the prison space (Epstein et al, 2022). Baldwin's (2022a, 2022b) research highlighted how, long before most of the mothers entered prison, there had often been multiple missed opportunities to support mothers differently. These missed and lost opportunities were often about responses to trauma, mental health, abuse, poverty and addictions, but significantly also around pregnancy, new motherhood and motherhood more generally. Torchalla et al (2014), in their study with women struggling with substance use during pregnancy and early motherhood, highlighted how participants had 'experienced multiple and continuing forms of adversities and trauma, often in form of gender-based violence, in a variety of contexts, from a variety of offenders and on multiple levels' (O'Malley et al, 2022: 3). As previously noted, and as argued by Clarke and Chadwick (2018), the focus of the CJS is too often to punish the individual, rather than understand or challenge the system which inflicts harm on women in contact with the CJS. This is despite the fact the 'offender' will almost certainly have been failed multiple times and by multiple agencies (Baldwin, 2015, 2021a, 2022a).

Often the missed opportunities are intergenerational, and opportunities for support and guidance originate from a childhood in which multiple disadvantages co-exist. Thus, in many instances had the mothers been appropriately supported much earlier, they might never have gone to prison or become criminalised at all.

Experiences of being mothered

Baldwin (2021a: 155) found that as well as the aforementioned challenges, many of the mothers in her study experienced a 'lack of mothering by mothers impoverished by their own circumstances', and that this had an effect on their mental wellbeing, their own ability to mother and their outcomes (and those of their children). Some mothers in both Baldwin and Abbott's research had experienced their own mother's imprisonment as children, and the impact of this was not lost on the mothers in the research. Stewart (2015) reiterates the importance of recognising the significance of mothers' own experiences of being mothered. She argues that for many criminalised mothers this bears some relationship to their life chances and choices, and their own ability to mother. Having the experience of being mothered by mothers who are living in disadvantage and challenging circumstances, or who might be distracted, addicted or abusive, can have a lifelong impact on a child. However, Stewart argues, it is important not to lay the blame for such experiences solely in the laps of the mothers, but rather on 'a society that fails to support them' (Stewart, 2015: 173). Hackett echoes Stewart and suggests that oftentimes when a mother is not able to mother 'well', it is not always because of personal or individual failure, but because 'they are often disadvantaged as a result of discrimination, inequality, weakened socio-economic positions and victimisation' (Hackett, 2015: 46). Mothers in such circumstances are nonetheless judged, blamed and othered (Baldwin, 2017, 2021a, 2021b). It is true that there cannot be effective criminal justice without effective social justice and as such it is vital that families, and perhaps especially mothers, are supported sooner to avoid the negative impact of a lack of support and disadvantage becoming intergenerational.

Baldwin co-wrote a chapter in *Criminal Women: Gender Matters* (Baldwin et al, 2022a) with two criminalised mothers who described their pre-prison circumstances and experience of maternal imprisonment. In the chapter Mary Elwood[1] described powerfully and vividly her pre-prison life. Mary experienced a traumatic and troubled childhood in which violent and sexual exploitation were present. Mary describes how she felt ill-equipped to make 'good choices' and fell into abusive and coercive situations as a young adult, after leaving home at 15. Her mother was an alcoholic and a sex worker. Mary described how she never felt loved or wanted by her mother (who was living within her own challenges), something Mary felt had an impact on her self-worth and her identity.

> When I was born, I can't imagine that my mother loved me even then. I often think about babies that are planned and wanted; I think they must know, the babies I mean. I think they must feel loved even before they were born. I see pregnant mothers stroking their full bellies and talking, even singing to their baby, excited about their child's life to come. I genuinely can't imagine my mother ever having done that with me. I was unplanned, an inconvenience, an unwanted interruption of her life and her 'work'. I'm sure I would have gotten in the way of her work save for those perverts who like pregnant working girls. It makes me feel dirty even now knowing my mum must have been paid for her body to be used with me inside it. I feel like I must have absorbed some of that dirt, some of that shame. I've read that science says that unborn babies pick up on their mothers' moods so it stands to reason I must have picked up on some of what was going on. I know bonding can start before babies are born, so I guess so can indifference, and that's what I always felt my mother felt about me. (Mary in Baldwin et al, 2022a: 110)

Living in a 'circle of circumstance'

Mary goes on to describe a childhood and life not untypical of many criminalised mothers. She describes her childhood with an alcoholic, emotionally unavailable mother and a violent stepfather. Mary left home at a very young age, straight into violent, abusive relationships. Mary became pregnant by her abusive partner who used threats to the welfare of her child to coerce her into offending. Mary began to use alcohol as a means of coping with her stressful and painful life and to 'block out' traumatic memories from her past (childhood rape). Like Mary, several mothers in Baldwin and Abbott's research spoke of how their maternal experiences were intertwined with their offending and criminalisation (and desistance), particularly those mothers who were using substances. Many of the mothers in the studies were living in what Baldwin calls 'a Circle of Circumstance' (see Figure 3.1), which included poverty, surviving trauma, mental ill-health, ongoing/past abuse and damaging relationships. For several of the mothers, despite the additional challenges it brought, becoming a mother was a positive for them, sometimes the only positive in their lives, and was something (sometimes the *only* thing) that many of the mothers felt they were "good at" (Beth). However, mothering in the context of addiction, trauma from past or ongoing abuse and/or in poverty is challenging, and, as described by many of the mothers, was incredibly difficult, stressful and guilt-inducing (Ghate and Hazel, 2002): "Sometimes just being alive was hard. I was so wrapped up in trying to cope with my past it was hard to live in the present you know … hard to be the mum I should be" (Beth).

Mothers in Baldwin's study (like most criminalised women), described how there had often been a core trauma or a significant traumatic event (or series of events), frequently dating back to childhood for which they had not been fully or appropriately supported (like Mary). As such, for some of the mothers, using substances as a means of coping with or blocking out the trauma became their 'normal'.

'I hated the fact I'd become my mother; I needed alcohol to cope with everything … everything from my past and actually everything I was living in … it blocked it out, dulled the pain. … I tried counselling but that literally did my head in ... pardon the pun ... so I just went back to drinking.' (Mary)

Not unusually, a lifestyle featuring substance use can become embedded with an 'offending' lifestyle – either because of a need to fund an addiction, or as a result of the often-chaotic lifestyles and relationships that accompany addiction. In our research it was certainly clear that there had often been multi-agency failures around supporting mothers appropriately in the original and subsequent traumas, but sometimes there was also a reluctance on the mothers' parts to actively seek help. Mothers living on the edges of the CJS, in fact any mother who feels she is not living up to the widely accepted internal and external ideals and ideology of motherhood (Baldwin, 2015), feels judged and subject to both formal and informal scrutiny. This impacted on the mothers' willingness to seek help and support. The mothers' reluctance was underpinned by several factors such as a suspicion of authority figures, negative past experiences and a lack of trust in services. However, the biggest and most absolute fear was that they might lose their children as result of asking for help. This meant that mothers often only came to the attention of CJS and social justice agencies at the point of crisis (see Figure 3.1). "I really wanted help but knew if I asked then the spotlight would really be on me, and I just didn't want to risk losing my kids" (Shanice).

Thus, for the mothers in our research, the stakes were high, and for those who did try to seek help and to secure support for their complex needs, they knew that they were doing this while trying to navigate their way through systems that at every turn had the *potential* to remove their children.

Cycles of trauma

For several of the mothers in our research, this meant that any support or intervention came late or too late, during a 'crisis', maybe on arrest, maybe a GP or social services referral and

Figure 3.1: Motherhood interrupted: cycle of criminalisation and child removal

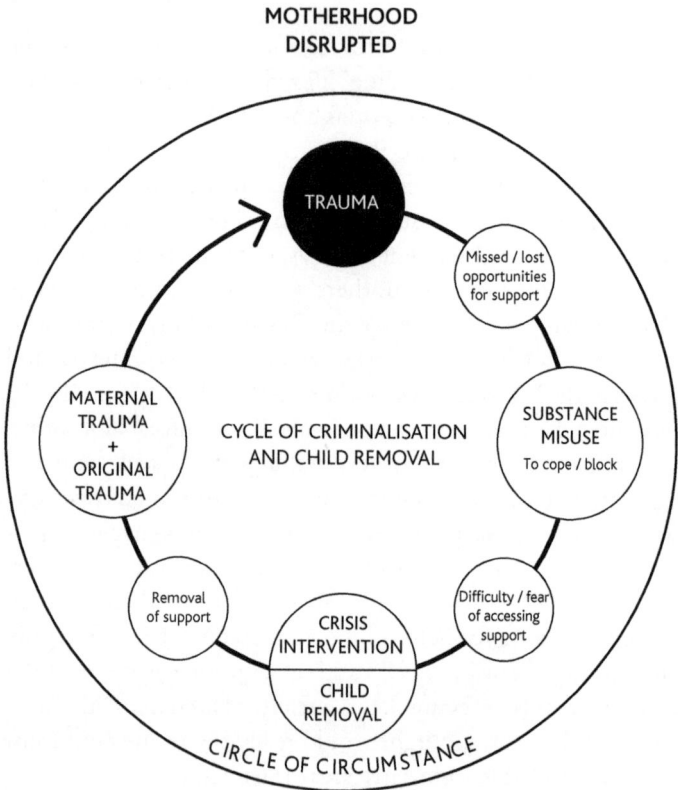

MOTHERHOOD
DISRUPTED

TRAUMA

Missed / lost opportunities for support

MATERNAL TRAUMA + ORIGINAL TRAUMA

CYCLE OF CRIMINALISATION AND CHILD REMOVAL

SUBSTANCE MISUSE
To cope / block

Removal of support

CRISIS INTERVENTION

CHILD REMOVAL

Difficulty / fear of accessing support

CIRCLE OF CIRCUMSTANCE

Source: Baldwin (2022b: 16–20)

sometimes triggered by routine pregnancy/antenatal care. This crisis point and subsequent intervention might be the point at which a mother comes into contact with the CJS or with social services through external referrals, as opposed to self-referral. The potential, consequential chain of events is reflected in Figure 3.1, and highlights the tautological situation many pregnant and/or criminalised women have found themselves in. The cycle is often repeated with mothers losing multiple children to the care system, sometimes at birth; all too often, at least in part, because the mother is not adequately (if at all) supported post-separation. This leads to more maternal trauma and not infrequently another pregnancy, which is often a heartbroken mother's attempt to 'redeem' herself, by recovering a maternal identity and role, *and* as a means of healing her maternal loss and trauma. This now additional maternal trauma is of course then 'on top' of the original trauma, and for some mothers now as well as the pre-existing addiction issues that influenced the offending and were a means of coping. With every child removal there is an increased risk of the loss of future children (Barnes, 2015), and an ever more deepening reluctance on the mothers' part to ask for help or engage with services. This reluctance is rooted in the very real fear of losing further children: "Why would I tell them I was struggling? Why … so they can take my kids again, no way" (Shanice). Thus, a 'crisis' point is reached again and the cycle repeats. For some mothers the cycle is perpetuated, and multiple child removals occur, causing ever more maternal trauma. The cycle illustrated here is relevant for mothers at all stages of their criminal justice journey because they could be 'trapped' in the cycle before, during and/or after prison.

Further illustrating this phenomenon, Mary described in her narrative how she was reluctant to ask for help either as a pregnant and/or new mother, despite the awful circumstances she was living in and an awareness that she needed help. Mary's downward spiral continued and eventually she was caught moving drugs for her abusive partner. Her toddler son was taken into care when she was remanded into custody, and she found she was pregnant on her reception into prison. Mary was released at seven months' pregnant, but after again being forced by her controlling partner to take drugs into a prison, she was very quickly back in prison with a baby due any day. Mary knew that her second son would be taken into care as soon as he was born.

I knew my son would be taken as soon as he was born. All I had left was to make the most of the couple of weeks I had left with him inside me. I must be only mum in the world who was delighted her baby was late. Every moment was precious and meant he was mine for longer, just me and him in our bubble – I barely even noticed I was in prison. (Mary in Baldwin et al, 2022a: 112)

As shown in the 'Motherhood Disrupted' cycle (Figure 3.1), Mary was now living with her original trauma from childhood, the additional trauma and experiences of her abusive relationships and now her maternal trauma, for which, without her children, Mary felt there was no healing from. Mary initially had hope she would get her boys back in her care when she was released, and as a result she was 'determined' to 'go straight'. For Mary (and many others), her children were her motivation (Abbott, 2018; Baldwin, 2022a; Bozkurt, 2022). Although Mary did eventually get her sons back in her care, her unresolved trauma, the added guilt and maternal trauma, and the lack of any ongoing support, meant that Mary soon fell into another damaging and violent relationship. She resorted to her "old coping mechanism", alcohol, and in a drunken state attacked her partner. Mary was jailed and her sons were placed in long-term foster care. When Mary was released, without any realistic prospect of getting her children back "anytime soon", Mary's downward spiral continued. She became fixed in a cycle of alcohol–offending–prison. She served many short prison sentences and felt that her situation was hopeless.

I got out eventually, no money, no home, no job and no kids. What was even the point in trying to stay sober [without them]. In my view my destiny had been decided when I was born my mother's child. So really the next ten years are a blur, in and out of prison drunk and sober, mostly drunk. Lots of short prison sentences for stupid things, sometimes just three weeks. I felt like I was on a conveyor belt – the officers would laugh when I came back and say 'you again' – I felt like a joke, everything felt inevitable. There didn't seem to any point even trying without my kids, I didn't see my boys at all. My boys were in care I had no fixed address most of the time so the social lost contact with me. I have to be honest and say I tried not to think about them, they were better off without me and really that part of my life was over. What use was I as a mother anyway no way would I have wanted them to see me like that, I'd seen my mother like that, and it wasn't pretty. So, I was happy imagining them with a good mum and dad in a nice area with a nice school and doing well. They were in a much better place, and I was glad. The only downside was I needed to drink to blot out the pain of it all, which mean robbing to pay for it. So that was my life year after year. (Mary in Baldwin et al, 2022a: 116)

Motherhood, motivation and desistance

Striking in Mary's description of her pre-prison life is that it isn't that different to many other criminalised mothers. It is not unusual for mothers who lose the care of their children to press what some call their "fuck it button" (Emma), meaning that without their children they have no will or motivation to cease offending, address any issues or desist from substance misuse. Pitman et al (2021) echoed this finding in their report into 'maternal imprisonment'. Significantly, any support, particularly from social services, mothers were previously accessing (if at all) is often withdrawn once their children are removed (Barnes, 2015). Until very recently there was little recognition of the relationship motherhood has to desistance or to how well (or not) mothers engage with prison or probation supervision (Baldwin, 2022a). Thus, the failures of the system to actively support mothers has a huge impact on mothers and their children, and opportunities to enable mothers to break cycles are once again lost. Bachman et al (2016) have argued that while obviously motherhood in and of itself does not inhibit offending behaviour (as this prosocial role did not prevent criminalised mothers from offending in the first instance), echoing Opsal (2011), they argue instead that 'when offenders are ready to adopt a prosocial identity, reclaiming their role as mother may indeed serve to solidify mothers' desired change' (Bachman et al, 2016: 215). However, this is often dependent on support, guidance and a reliance on the courts to make good decisions for women and mothers who appear before them.

Pause for thought

- How are you feeling about the mothers?
- Do you think they can mother 'well' in circumstances like those previously described?
- What could/should be put in place by way of support?
- What are the barriers to support?
- What could you do?
- How does mothers' experiences relate to their offending?

The criminal justice response to pregnant and new mothers

Baroness Corston's (2007) report sought to generate responses to criminalised women that would help create a 'distinct, radically different, visibly led, strategic, proportionate, holistic, women centred, integrated approach' (Corston, 2007: 79). The 43 recommendations of the Corston report reiterated the need for positive change concerning women and criminal justice, echoing researchers, academics and practitioners who had called for such changes for more than 30 years (Carlen, 1985; 2004; Gelsthorpe and Morris, 2002). Corston's report generated great optimism, achieving cross-party support, and is widely seen as a 'roadmap for women specific criminal justice reform' (Baldwin and Epstein, 2017: 7). Central to the report was the message that far fewer women ought to be sentenced to custody, and that prison ought to be reserved only for the very few women who pose a danger to the public, with community-based 'alternatives to custody' sought wherever possible, obviously this related to pregnant and new mothers also. Women in Prison found in its 'Corston Plus ten'[2] report that despite widespread support for the Corston recommendations, and some real progress in some key areas, none of Corston's recommendations have been fully implemented and the female prison population remains 'stubbornly high'.[3] Women, including pregnant and new mothers, continue to be sent to prison either on remand or at sentence;[4] despite consistent evidence that community sentences are more appropriate, more effective and less harmful to both mothers and children. Custodial sentences continue to be imposed for low-level offences such as shoplifting, or for breach of a court order (often for an original offence, that would not have attracted a custodial sentence in the first instance).

The Female Offender Strategy (2018) and the Female Focused Farmer Review (2019) echo Corston, both stating that the imprisonment of women, particularly for short sentences, and for those who have committed nonviolent crimes, should be avoided in favour of community alternatives. Nonetheless, despite widespread misgivings about short sentences, their use has continued to rise. In 1993 only a third of custodial sentences given to women were for less than six months, while in 2020 it was almost three in five (58 per cent) (PRT, 2022: 38). In 2019, 35 per cent of women in prison were sentenced for a first offence (Pitman et al, 2021). The Prison Reform Trust found that community sentences for women have declined by two-thirds in a decade. The Criminal Justice Act 2003 states that imposing a custodial sentence must only occur when an offence is 'so serious that no other alternative can be justified', yet more than 70 per cent of women sentenced to custody are convicted of nonviolent offences. Many women are in prison on remand, not yet found guilty of anything, and most of these women (over 70 per cent) then go on to be given a non-custodial sentence, bringing into question the logic or necessity of their remand, especially if those women were pregnant or separating from very young babies and children. Until very recently official statistics around the sentencing of pregnant and new mothers were not collated, as such mothers/ women are invisible within this statistical context. As are their young children and breastfeeding babies (Baldwin and Epstein, 2017; PRT, 2022).

Sentencing guidelines

The context described in the previous section occurs despite there being existing guidance and requirements to consider alternatives to custody in the case of pregnant and new mothers. In 2010, the UK signed up to The United Nations Rules for the Treatment of Women Prisoners and Non-Custodial Measures for Women Offenders (the Bangkok Rules[5]). These, among others, include provisions and guidance for the sentencing of mothers, including pregnant and new mothers. Rules 48–52 of the Bangkok Rules are specific and can be summarised as follows.

The imprisonment of a parent involves the forcible separation of parent and child and as such activates the Article 8[11] (European Convention on Human Rights 1950 [ECHR]) rights of the child by 'depriving the child of parental care'. Thus, when sentencing mothers (and fathers) of dependent children the courts are 'guided' to acquire information about dependent children; and balance the Article 8 rights of the child against the seriousness of the mother's offence and the impact of a custodial sentence on the children separated from their mother. Ultimately, to make a 'balanced' decision about whether prison is the most appropriate option. This applies to all the countries that have ratified the ECHR' (Epstein, 2021). In a precedent-setting case (*R (on the application of P and Q)* v *Secretary of State for the Home Department* [2001]

EWCA Civ 1151), the Court of Appeal heard a challenge made by two mothers on an MBU concerning inflexibility of the age of forced separation from their babies at 18 months. Lord Philips (Master of the Rolls), in his consideration of the appeal, questioned as to why the mothers had been sentenced to custody in the first instance, and stated:

> It goes without saying that since 2nd October 2000 sentencing courts have been public authorities within the meaning of section 6 of the Human Rights Act. If the passing of a custodial sentence involves the separation of a mother from her very young child (or, indeed, from any of her children) the sentencing court is bound ... to carry out the balancing exercise ... before deciding that the seriousness of the offence justifies the separation of mother and child. If the court does not have sufficient information about the likely consequences of the compulsory separation, it must, in compliance with its obligations under section 6(1), ask for more. (Epstein, 2011: 12)

Lord Phillips stated that, in sentencing a mother with dependent children, the rights of the child have to be weighed against the seriousness of the offence in a 'balancing exercise'. This judgment made clear that magistrates and judges must (1) acquire information about dependent children; and (2) balance the Article 8 rights of the child against the seriousness of the mother's offence (Epstein, 2011: 12; see also Epstein, 2021). Yet despite this guidance women, including pregnant women and new mothers, continue to be sentenced and remanded to custody, often with insufficient consideration of their context or the appropriateness of custody as a disposal.

In 2011 Epstein sought to find out if this 'balancing exercise' described previously does take place. Epstein analysed the cases of 75 mothers. Of the 75 cases, five were heard in magistrates' courts, 31 in Crown Courts and 39 in the Court of Appeal. Three of the cases resulted in Community Orders, 51 were sentences of immediate imprisonment and 19 attracted suspended sentences. In seven of the 51 cases of immediate custody, Epstein (2011) found that the sentencers made *no mention* of the defendant's dependent children at all. In other cases, judges acknowledged the children's likely suffering and misery on the imposition of a prison sentence but laid the responsibility for the situation on the mothers themselves. Overall, none of the cases that resulted in immediate custody appeared to have the balancing exercise carried out (Bozkurt, 2022). Similarly, Minson (2020), who also undertook research around 'Maternal sentencing and the rights of the child', found that the rights of the child and the impact of maternal imprisonment were inconsistently and inadequately applied at the point of sentencing. Furthermore, Minson (2020) found that the welfare of the child was considered differently between the family courts and the criminal courts, with far greater weight given concerning forced separation in the family courts. When considering the evidence of the authors' research and that of others it is clear that the criminalisation of the mothers brings questions over her 'character' and 'good mother status' (Baldwin, 2022a), and as such may be a factor in the lack of care and consideration sometimes given to the separation from her children (Masson, 2019; Bozkurt, 2022).

Minson (2020) and Baldwin (2022a), as well as others (Masson, 2019; Booth, 2020; Pitman et al, 2021), found that judges often did not consider, or even ask, if a woman had dependent children. Pre-sentence reports are not always requested, but even when they are they are not always bound to show information about children or how they would be cared for if the mother was imprisoned. Custodial sentences are not necessarily anticipated by the women, and in fact sometimes they may have been advised that because they are mothers, or because of the lack of seriousness of their offence, they would avoid prison sentences. As a result, they may not have identified who could and would look after their children if they were sentenced to prison.

Progress?

Following a recommendation from the Joint Human Rights Committee report on 'The right to family life: Children whose mothers are in prison' (an inquiry to which both authors submitted written and oral evidence), in October 2019, a new sentencing guideline was issued by the Sentencing Council. The additional guidance included an expanded explanation for the mitigating factor 'sole or primary carer for dependent relatives' as described earlier. Within the list of 'factors reducing seriousness or reflecting personal mitigation' housed in the 'Sentencing Guidelines', 'sole or primary carer for dependent relatives' is listed, however now an expanded explanation of the factor is included. Since its first inclusion in a sentencing guideline in 2011 until 2019, there has not been a clear explanation as to how this factor should be considered within sentencing decisions, resulting in inconsistency of approach, especially in the magistrates' courts, alongside the common failure to uphold children's rights when mothers (and fathers) are sentenced. The additional guidance asks the court to consider the impact that a custodial sentence of their parent would have on the children. It asks the court to consider an adjournment for care arrangements to be made if custody is deemed the only appropriate disposal, and it asks the court to request a Pre-sentence Report from the probation service to outline dependents and their needs. It is important to add that the additional guidance specifically mentions pregnant mothers and/or their unborn children, who also have rights (O'Malley et al, 2022). The additional guidance states, 'when the defendant is a pregnant woman the relevant considerations should include the effect of a sentence of imprisonment on the woman's health and any effect of the sentence on the unborn child'. Importantly, the additional guidance also states that 'the court should not impose a sentence of imprisonment where the impact on dependents would make a custodial sentence disproportionate to achieving the aims of sentencing'. It is clear that any sentence that would result in maternal separation, perhaps particularly if the dependents are very young, or it will mean a baby being born to a mother in prison or residing on an MBU for the first months of its life, would add an additional layer of punishment and potentially harm, and that, in most cases, would be disproportionate to the offence committed (O'Malley et al, 2021).

In practice?

In 2022, Epstein et al published their report *Why are Pregnant Women in Prison?* They found that despite the guidance outlined previously, women are still being sentenced, remanded and recalled for minor and very minor offences, while pregnant or as mothers of children under two years old. In their study of mothers who were between five and 36 weeks pregnant when sentenced, Epstein et al (2022) found that oftentimes very little consideration was given to the mothers' contexts or backgrounds, and as discussed earlier many of the mothers were living with multiple challenges like poverty, mental ill-health, addition and abuse. Indicatively, Epstein et al cite a press reference to a magistrate speaking to a pregnant defendant who had not fully complied with probation conditions: 'I would lose no sleep sending a pregnant woman to prison.' Epstein et al argue vociferously for a change in both social attitudes and the law (Epstein et al, 2022: 5).

Minoritised women must deal with racism and prejudice on several levels, which may be both traumatising and harmful, possibly impeding normal growth and functioning in individuals who are subjected to it (Bozkurt, 2022), and it is important to note that Black, Asian and ethnic minority women will also already be facing similar challenges as White British women. Research shows Black, Asian and ethnic minority women's experiences of criminal justice and maternity systems are characterised by disparities (Epstein et al, 2022), and furthermore ethnically minoritised women are more likely than other women to be remanded or sentenced to custody (Bozkurt and Thomas, 2023). Research has further shown that minoritised women have a higher risk of pregnancy complications, miscarriage and stillbirth, and a higher risk of death in childbirth, all of which have further implications for the care and experiences of minoritised women in prison (MBRRACE-UK: Mothers and Babies: Reducing Risk through Audits and Confidential Enquiries). The recent PPO reports into the deaths of Baby A and Baby B have called for all pregnant women in prison to be categorised as 'high risk' in recognition of the complex needs associated with women in prison. However, we argue that simply classifying imprisoned mothers and their pregnancies as high risk will do little to alter the challenges of the environment and that in fact we revert to our original argument that wherever possible pregnant and new mothers should be in the community.

Pause for thought

- What is your view on pregnancy and motherhood as a mitigating factor in sentencing?
- Do you think a mother committing crime is viewed more harshly than women who are not mothers in society/in courts?
- Do you think prisons are a safe place to be pregnant?

The mothers' voices: experiences of arrest and sentencing

Mothers in both the authors' research described variable experiences, again highlighting the inconsistency with which pregnant and new mothers are treated. Some mothers described being responded to with compassion, sensitivity and kindness, however for others any care or consideration was lacking, and a few of the mothers felt they were treated deliberately harshly and unkindly *because* they were mothers or were pregnant. It is worth noting that both authors have spoken to women whose sentencers told them in court that they would be 'safer' and better cared for in prison as pregnant mothers than they were 'outside', this reasoning in part to justify a custodial sentence where one might otherwise not have been imposed. One mother, in the last few weeks of pregnancy, was apparently told 'I would prefer the thought of you giving birth behind bars, than on the street.'

From Baldwin's research, Beth was still breastfeeding her three-month-old baby when she was arrested late at night in her home, and she describes the devastation and the upset when her daughter was wrenched from her arms before she was taken away. Beth describes 'begging' officers to let her feed her baby 'one last time' before they would be separated.

> I was feeding her, and she was looking up at me with these totally innocent eyes ... she had no idea what was coming and honestly my tears were just dripping all over her face, but she had no idea ... no idea ... just innocent. I was broken ... I still am, I think about that all the time. (Beth in Baldwin, 2022a: 247)

Beth was not advised that she could have applied for an MBU space on her arrival at the prison and so her baby was taken immediately into care. The outside social workers refused to allow the baby to visit the prison and Beth did not see her baby for the whole of her sentence. Beth's story and the impact of this decision will be revisited in the following chapter. Dee, who was a mother of four children, with two under two years when she was sentenced to immediate custody, absconded from the courtroom just so that she could take her baby to her sisters and hopefully avoid her baby being taken into care. She recalls, 'all I could think about was getting there and getting them to my sisters ... it was mad, but I had to' (Dee in Baldwin, 2022a: 247). Dee described how this memory of her running would often trouble her dreams, where she would just be running and running but never getting anywhere and she relates this to trying to get to her children, 'it's a memory and a living nightmare at the same time' (Dee in Baldwin, 2022a: 278). Similarly, Shanice, who like Beth was arrested at home, remembers running out of the back door as the police were knocking on the front door, running with her baby in her arms to take her to a neighbour, again so her baby would not be immediately taken into care. Bozkurt (2022), in her research with ethnically minoritised mothers, describes a still breastfeeding mother's trauma when she was sentenced to immediate custody and taken down to the holding cells, 'they had me in handcuffs and it was disgusting but I was crying and telling my barrister my son, I still breastfeed, my baby, where's my baby' (Sadia in Bozkurt, 2022: 98). Bozkurt (2022) describes how the trauma of separation caused Sadia to be unable to process what had happened to her, and states that Sadia kept asking 'where's my baby' even though she knew where her baby was. Sadia described to Bozkurt how she felt before court (not expecting a custodial sentence) and on her immediate reception into custody:

I remember specifically saying goodbye to my son. I kissed him and breastfed him in the morning. I had this horrible thought that this might be the last time I get to hold him ... I thought I was going to die, like physically the pain I felt ... I remember my breast was filled up with milk, so I had to stand by the sink and literally milk myself and it was so painful, I was crying ... this is all the milk that my baby should be drinking. (Sadia in Bozkurt, 2022: 98)

Bozkurt describes how Sadia's guilt at disposing of milk meant for her son was incredibly damaging to her. It is not difficult to imagine the fear and trauma of the mothers, and importantly the babies, in situations such as these.

Conversely, Abbott's research describes the experiences of other mothers for whom their pregnancy seemed irrelevant in their sentencing, despite the aforementioned guidance. For some mothers their pregnancy wasn't mentioned at court, therefore it was not mitigated for, and as such then this had an impact on how this mother was received and responded to in prison.

> The people in court forgot I was pregnant. They didn't bring a special van for me, which is something they were supposed to have done. I got to (Prison X) and they were like, 'What the hell are you doing here? You weren't supposed to come here, you were supposed to go somewhere else'. But, obviously, they can't arrange that transport from there, so what was meant to be like a one-week pit stop to take me somewhere else, ended up being until I was in labour. (Sammy in Abbott, 2018: 85)

Some mothers were advised by their legal counsel not to mention their motherhood or even pregnancy in court (Baldwin, 2022a). Abbott (2018: 92–93) describes a mother whose 'extreme emotional reaction to being sentenced' meant that she was 'threatened with psychiatric treatment'. Abbott quotes Sammy as saying:

> I just assumed that from court I'd be taken to a mother and baby unit. … And I wasn't, so when I was in a little bit of a hysterical fit just after being sentenced, I just had a bit of a breakdown. And then you get told you better sort yourself out, otherwise they'll put you on a funny wing, so you have to be strong from that moment. That's the only way that you can cope with it. (Sammy in Abbott, 2018: 93)

Abbott (2018) describes the unbelievable and horrific experience of Sylvia. Sylvia was sentenced to immediate custody at 41 weeks. Sylvia went into labour in the court but was still transported to prison. Sylvia was sent straight to hospital from the prison reception where she gave birth, she was forcibly separated from her baby and returned to the prison without her baby – all within a 24-hour period. It is not difficult to imagine the impact this had on Sylvia (and her baby), and importance of her trauma being recognised and her being fully supported.

Given the close mother–child bond, particularly during the child's early weeks and months while breastfeeding, this 'forced separation' (Baldwin, 2017) can be significantly traumatic and physically agonising and can in fact have lifelong health and wellbeing implications (Thornburg et al, 2014; see also Egeland and Farber, 1984; Baradon et al, 2008; Redshaw and Martin, 2013).

Awareness of mother and baby units

'Paige' (speaking to Baldwin in 2023), became pregnant while waiting for her case to come to court. She describes painful memories of initially thinking she would have to have to abort her much loved and much wanted baby because she "simply had no idea babies could go to prison with their mothers" (Paige). Later, knowing she personally would never be able to abort her baby, Paige was traumatised instead with thoughts that she would have to "hand her baby out" as soon as she was born.

> 'It was a gut-wrenching thought but I as far as I knew it was our only option. Who would our daughter call mumma? It was hard to grip. But some women are not in my position some don't have loving families to support them, this means their options are more limited some of them believe terminating their pregnancy is the only way.' (Paige)

Paige found the process bewildering, frightening and stressful and she worried about the impact all of the stress, the worry about her sentencing and beyond, would have on her baby. Paige describes how professionals failed to advise and guide her, and it felt "almost as if I wasn't even pregnant" at times. Paige was sentenced to imprisonment 11 days before her due date. She felt that it would have been so much less stressful if she had known about her options. She states:

'You find out all this information BUT too late, when you are no longer a woman facing their sentence pregnant. The information needs to be present in police cells, because ultimately that is the first point of criminal proceedings. Hospitals, court rooms, GP surgeries, and solicitors. All have a part to play in supporting women with ALL of their options.' (Paige)

Paige regards herself as 'lucky' that on reception into prison she was told about the MBU and her eligibility to apply. Thankfully, she was treated compassionately and speedily and although she was sentenced on a Friday the prison managed to have an emergency MBU board and Paige was advised on the following Tuesday that she had her place, and she would be able to keep her daughter with her. As highlighted in Chapters One and Five, this is not always the case (Sikand, 2015; Trowler, 2022). In another prison Paige might have had an agonising wait for the board or her baby may have been removed from her care temporarily while the board was arranged, and a decision was made. A situation which can, and has, for some mothers, taken weeks and sometimes only occurred after birth (Sikand, 2015; Abbott, 2018, 2022).

Abbott's research also described mothers not knowing about the existence of MBUs and the possibility of their babies coming into prison with them:

I didn't know there was a mother and baby unit, I didn't know the ins and outs of the MBU, it was the other prisoners that told me that there was a Mother and

Baby Unit and that you can apply for it. And none of the officers spoke to me about it, nothing, I just had to go off and do it all myself. (Layla in Abbott, 2018: 86)

However, it is important to remember that even when mothers are aware of an MBU and are able to apply in a timely manner, not all mothers will be approved for a space, and many will be forcibly separated from their babies at birth (Sikand, 2015). Abbott is currently researching the experiences of mothers separated from their babies in this way, with findings expected to be published in 2024/2025.

Conclusion

As this chapter has shown, when mothers become criminalised it is rarely without a broader context of challenges. Many women who come into contact with the CJS, including pregnant and new mothers, have faced multiple challenges, many are victims of crime, have experienced abuse, mental health and/or substance misuse issues, poverty and disadvantage. There have often been missed and lost opportunities to support mothers, which had they not been missed may well have contributed to a different, more positive, outcome for the mothers and their babies.

It is clear from our and others' research (Sikand, 2015; Epstein et al, 2022) that despite guidance and provision in sentencing frameworks and statute, pregnant and new mothers have varied experiences at the point of arrest, in court and in their reception into prison. Entering prison as a pregnant woman is hard enough but entering as a pregnant woman not knowing your rights or entitlements is especially distressing. Similarly, entering prison as a mother, perhaps especially a mother of a baby, is incredibly traumatising. If we are to still send pregnant and new mothers to prison, and as we have stated our preferred option is that we do not, then women like the women in this chapter must be advised, guided and most importantly understood and supported through what will be, for most, the most awful time in their lives.

Through the eyes and voices of the mothers, and drawing from our research, the following two chapters (Chapters Four and Five) will focus on mothers in prison and post-prison experiences.

FOUR

Motherhood confined

'Walking round in a prison with a huge bump, I can't think of anything that could make you feel more ashamed.'

Michelle, 2022

Introduction

This chapter, drawing on the authors' respective qualitative research, will discuss mothers' experiences of pregnancy and new motherhood in prison. In this chapter we specifically explore issues around access to basic needs, explicitly antenatal support, appropriate nutrition, experiences of external appointments in local hospitals, and birth as an imprisoned mother. It will detail in the mothers' voices what it feels like to be a pregnant or new mother in prison. It also explores the significance of the reactions of prison staff and the mothers' relationships with one another. The chapter will centre the women's voices and experiences as described to us. Mothers in our respective research focused their responses on several key areas – stress and safety; shame; antenatal care and experiences of external appointments; food; miscarriage and cell births; and living on an MBU – and these inform the structure of this chapter.

Early days in prison

Several mothers in our research described the shock and horror they felt at being sentenced to prison, and for some the prison sentence was unexpected. As Baldwin (2021a) highlights, these early days are a risky time for mothers and mothers-to-be. The risk of suicide and self-harm in those first few hours and days is heightened. Sometimes the prison is aware of this and will account for this in their care and observations, as described by Jane:

> When I was sentenced, I was so shocked I cried 'I prefer to be dead than go to prison' and you know when you say these things, they put me on suicide watch. I had to shake a leg every hour! Every hour for two weeks, I had to shake my leg every hour to show I was still alive. (Jane in Abbott, 2018: 102)

The care put in place for pregnant women and new mothers was generally in the form of security protocols or procedures, such as opening ACCT documents to keep women from self-harm. However, rather than this feeling like a support mechanism for women, being 'on suicide watch' – as one woman exclaimed, "having a light shone in my eyes every 15 minutes through the night" – was distressing, especially for those returning to prison following separation. Women would sometimes talk about how they would hide their emotions to avoid this scrutiny. Other pregnant or new mothers tried their best to manage their pain on their own, while often acknowledging that they felt suicidal. Beth, whose three-month-old baby was taken into her care at her arrest, stated: 'I just didn't want to be here anymore, I felt like I'd lost her [her baby] forever, if I wasn't a mother anymore what was the point of me?' (Beth in Baldwin, 2022a: 118).

Kady felt that it was only the fact than an officer "was kind" to her, and "made time" to support her as a newly pregnant mum, that she "got through that first week" (Baldwin, 2022a: 119). She felt if not for that officer she might have taken her life. Taranpreet, who was separated from her baby (who was with relatives), described feeling 'totally broken', as if she was 'dead inside'. She was convinced that her child would forget her, and she admitted those thoughts left her suicidal (Baldwin, 2022a: 118). The experiences of the mothers vividly highlight the importance of what Baldwin (2022a) calls 'maternal trauma' being recognised, understood and supported, throughout the criminal justice process, but perhaps especially in prison when mothers are at their most mentally vulnerable.

Prison as a safe space?

Research has demonstrated that pregnancy in prison is a painful experience full of negative emotions such as shame, anxiety, loss of a sense of self and disempowerment (Abbott et al, 2020). Although, as we have previously stated, we believe that almost all criminalised pregnant women would be more appropriately responded to by way of a community penalty, there is no doubt that for some women, entering the prison space can bring 'temporary relief' and can alleviate some aspects of a mother's previous 'circle of circumstance' (Baldwin, 2022b). While we believe that this is in many ways a reflection of the aforementioned 'missed and lost opportunities' for support, and lack of community-based resources (Baldwin, 2022b), we do appreciate that prison for *some* women can be a 'breathing space'. Some mothers spoke to us about feeling 'safer' at being away from abusive and violent partners. Although pregnancy in prison is far from ideal, we do acknowledge that for some mothers, particularly those living in challenging circumstances before prison, there are some reported positive experiences of connectedness (Wismont, 2000) and bonding with the unborn baby (Abbott, 2018). These positive experiences have been described as 'moments of quiet', usually at night when the unborn baby gives some comfort through kicks and movement, bringing with him/her a sense of companionship (Wismont, 2000; Abbott, 2018). Mary (mentioned in the previous chapter, and who will feature in later chapters too) found out she was pregnant on reception into prison and, although she knew her baby would be forcibly removed at birth, she described her incarcerated pregnancy as 'like a sanctuary'. For Mary unlike her previous pregnancy, that had been marred by violence, substance misuse and 'chaos'; it was a time for her to bond with her baby in a way that she had previously felt unable to. Mary spoke about 'loving' the 'peace and space' to be able 'stroke her belly and sing to her child', focusing on her baby, not the abusive circumstances she was living in outside (Mary in Baldwin et al, 2022a: 112). However, any bonding Mary felt was nonetheless experienced under the painful cloud and shadow of impending separation.

However, it must be said that if more could be done in the community to ensure all criminalised and vulnerable women had access to timely support and resources that were appropriately funded, then most women would routinely feel these normal bonding experiences – and perhaps they wouldn't be quite so extraordinary.

Other mothers in our research described no such quiet loving and bonding moments, and in fact some mothers felt their environment, their situation or the impending potential/inevitable separation from their baby was stopping them from bonding with their baby at all. For them there was nothing about prison that was a safe space: 'I was so concerned with keeping my belly safe in there I didn't really think about it as a baby or even me as a mam … so when the baby was born I felt quite disconnected. I didn't feel like he was even mine' (Tanisha in Baldwin, 2021b: 28).

Abbott described how the mothers in her study were preoccupied with the agony of impending separation and this brought up in them complicated and contrasting feelings, with the mothers' thoughts sometimes at odds with how they felt they should behave:

I'll have no bump and no baby. I don't know what I'm going to do ... how can anyone think it's natural to just take a baby away from their mum? (Caroline in Abbott, 2018: 161)

Hard, really hard, but there's nothing I can do about it ... so I have my moments, I'm upset, but just I'd rather to try and keep myself strong. (Susan in Abbott, 2018: 162)

Susan and Caroline described feeling stressed through most of their imprisoned pregnancy.

Stress and feeling 'unsafe'

In both Baldwin's and Abbott's research pregnant mothers described feeling 'stressed' and 'afraid' about experiencing a pregnancy behind bars, especially when it was their first baby.

I didn't feel safe in normal location, but I don't think I would have liked to have been on the MBU either, not when I didn't know if I'd get to even keep my baby. But it was awful being pregnant in prison, I felt unsafe, uncomfortable, hungry and upset ... all the time. (Tarian in Baldwin, 2022c: 27)

Abbott et al (2020) describe how mothers felt 'protective' over their bellies and worried about what would happen to them if they fell in the hostile environment of the prison, or if a fight broke out on the wing and they were harmed in an altercation. It is known that stress in pregnancy can and does have an impact on the unborn baby that can be long-lasting (Thornburg et al, 2014). Managing that stress and worrying about the impact on their babies was something else the mothers had to factor into their incarcerated pregnancy experience. The women were very aware that they 'should not' be 'stressing out' in order to prevent harm to their babies, but they felt intimidated by the environment and other prisoners. This placed some mothers in a perpetual state of hypervigilance. The impact of stress in pregnancy on the unborn baby was something the mothers worried could cause longer-term harm. Not an unreasonable fear (Thornburg et al, 2014; O'Malley et al, 2021). Mothers in both Abbott and Baldwin's studies attributed pregnancy issues and their child's physical health issues experienced post-birth to the stress they had experienced during their incarcerated pregnancies.

> He didn't grow properly; he was only five pounds six when he was born … he was two weeks early. He's got slight tongue tie, which I think is because of all the stress I was going through [in prison]. (Abbott, 2018: 95)

> He's got something wrong with him; I don't know if that's anything to do with the stress, my pregnancy being stressful. I think it probably did, because if the mum's stressed the child's stressed isn't it? (Abbott, 2018: 94)

Several mothers in our research spoke of their fears of losing their babies in prison, and in both our research we spoke to mothers who did miscarry in prison. In one of Baldwin's earlier studies (Baldwin and Epstein, 2017), two mothers felt the miscarriages they experienced in custody were directly related to the stress of being an imprisoned mother, something which added to the guilt already felt as a 'prison mother':

> I lost the baby in prison, and I will always believe that was down to the stress of being locked up – I'm certain I would have carried that baby if I'd been out – I still struggle with the guilt of it – I feel like I've killed my baby by getting sent to prison – I've had to have counselling to deal with it. (Baldwin and Epstein, 2017: 29)

Until very recently figures concerning miscarriage, termination and even pregnancy were not routinely collected (O'Keefe and Dixon, 2015; Abbott, 2018). The PPO has called for all pregnancies in prison to be treated as 'high risk' by virtue of the fact that an imprisoned pregnant woman is locked behind a door for a significant amount of time, which, in and of itself, is a stressful experience and one that carries risks. Several mothers in Abbott's study stated that the stress and fear came from worry that they might be a target for other prisoners' violence. Lola describes how she deliberately hid her belly to avoid any negative attention or violence:

> I've got baggy tops, so I just always have to hide my bump, and like most people couldn't recognize that I'm pregnant, so that's a good thing. So, I'm glad I'm not like, out here [gestures] I want it hidden, because I don't know who's who and who is in for what. (Lola in Abbott et al, 2020: 666)

Trixie, in Abbott's research, described having direct threats made to her and her baby, something other mothers had also described: 'she kept trying to push the door on me, and I just told her to go away, and she just kept saying that ... "I wish your baby dies"' (Trixie in Abbott, 2018: 74). Mothers described to us how the stress and fear of being pregnant in prison was also exacerbated by their 'guilt and shame' at being in prison as pregnant mothers.

Shame and being a 'pregnant prisoner'

Baldwin (2017) argues that many mothers enter prison 'already feeling they have failed as mothers, because of their lived experiences, their life chances and their life choices, which in turn has a significant impact on their self-esteem, maternal identity and maternal emotions' (Baldwin, 2017: 3).

Bozkurt (2022) argues the situation is then amplified for some minoritised mothers who also have to contend with experiences of racism and discrimination while imprisoned. Kady, a young Black mother in Baldwin's research, who entered prison pregnant, describes an experience that illustrates the point. Kady was supervised by a Black probation officer and on her release was told by her probation officer that she had 'let her race down'; she told Kady that as 'an intelligent black mother you should have been better, you have let us all down' (Baldwin, 2022a: 193). Kady described how this conversation played over in her head, interacting with her own already reducing self-esteem, specifically, her maternal self-esteem. For Kady, her guilt and shame was layered:

> I have never forgotten it. I was already questioning myself, could I do this, could I be a good role model to my daughter as a mother who'd been to prison? As a mother whose baby was born in prison. I was already questioning, man, and she went and said that … she said that! … so now I have to feel guilty not only as a mum … but as a black mum too. (Kady in Baldwin, 2022a: 193)

Black women and mothers, though over-represented in the CJS, are significantly under-represented in the literature, although Bozkurt (2022) and Thomas (2023) have recently completed important work around women, mothers and criminal justice that make an important contribution to the field. David Lammy found that for every White woman sentenced to prison for a drugs offence, 227 Black women were imprisoned for the same offence.[1] Clearly, this requires further investigation and examination. Interestingly, in Kady's words, 'bigger' than her 'black shame' was her 'motherhood shame': 'I dunno … it was like … aww man … like pregnancy is a pure time innit … becoming a mum. Its special … and to be in prison for it … I can't describe it. It just felt wrong … more wrong than if I weren't [pregnant]' (Kady in Baldwin, 2022c: 27).

Kady was not the only mother to speak about the shame of being a 'prison mother'. For many of the mothers in our research, the shame carried through the prison sentence and was still felt post-release (as will be discussed in the following chapter). Mothers described how the shame had sometimes begun in the courts, but it was in the prison space for many that it was at its most intense. Michelle, quoted at the outset of this chapter, goes on to describe how she "tried to hide my bump all the time, I didn't want the judgement from the officers, I was judging myself enough" (Michelle). Feeling stigmatised (Goffman, 1963) was a feeling many of the mothers described and for some their 'spoiled maternal identity' (Baldwin, 2022a: 190) was linked to fears of negative evaluation by others (Liss et al, 2013). Echoing Michelle, Tamika describes her feelings:

> I hate people knowing that I was pregnant both times I went to prison, it was bad enough being judged in court ... I think, well everyone thinks, it's worse being in prison pregnant ... so no I don't tell people if I can help it ... it's just wrong, innit, and those that I do tell or have told, well they just look down their noses at you ... it's like, 'how could you?'. You can see it in their eyes. It makes them question what kind of person you are. (Tamika in Baldwin, 2022a: 192)

Similarly, mothers in Baldwins' research who had been forced to leave their babies behind outside of prison, either in local authority care or with relatives, felt a shame directly related to their motherhood: 'Almost as soon as I went into the prison, I knew I would forever be looked at as a bad mother ... and I felt like one too to be fair ... there can't be much worse than a mother who goes to prison can there?' (Rita in Baldwin 2021a: 164).

Pregnant mothers in prison feel 'deprived' of a 'normal pregnancy experience', and this feeling of abnormality, of not being able to celebrate pregnancy or prepare for motherhood 'like normal pregnant mothers', also added to their sense of shame and difference. Bozkurt (2022) describes how a pregnant mother, Tanisha, in her study felt that she was not supported, and that she was denied access to 'normal' interventions for pregnancy discomforts like morning sickness. Bozkurt reports that Tanisha had not seen herself in a full-length mirror at all during her pregnancy and felt deprived by that:

> There were no mirrors, just a tiny one above the sink, so I never saw my body until I was in labour. Erm, I was growing, like my breasts, my belly and I didn't even know what I looked like. There were no opportunities to take photos, so I have no memories of that journey. (Tanisha in Bozkurt, 2022: 100)

Pause for thought

- Can you imagine what it might have been like to be pregnant in prison?
- What do you think you would find the hardest?
- Do you think the mothers are right to feel shame and guilt?

Antenatal care

Pregnant mothers in both Baldwin and Abbott's research described frustrations with their antenatal care, mostly around issues of access to equitable care (see also Chapter Six). Some mothers in our research did state that they engaged more fully with antenatal care in prison than they would have pre-prison – primarily because of the circumstances in which they were living. However, that cannot, and should not, ever be a reason to send a pregnant woman to prison.

Currently, although prison officers are tasked with the day-to-day care and safety of pregnant women in prison, midwives still provide antenatal care in prison. Midwives monitor the pregnancy and wellbeing of the women and visit the mothers after the baby is born in order to provide postnatal care. Midwives caring for imprisoned mothers are typically based in local community teams rather than with prison healthcare teams (Abbott, 2018). However, since the *Review of Operational Policy on Pregnancy, Mother and Baby Units and Maternal Separation* published in July 2022, all prisons are required to have a Pregnancy, Mother and Baby Liaison Officer (PMBLO). Also following the review, specialist midwives have an increased presence in the prisons, and some female prisons have a specialist prison midwife who leads a multidisciplinary team and who is responsible for the care and needs of all pregnant prisoners. Despite HMP Low Newton's aforementioned award-winning provision of a perinatal pathway (which includes a specialist prison midwife) being accepted as the 'gold standard' for prison antenatal and postnatal care, the full pathway is yet to be rolled out consistently across the estate. In 2022, Abbott founded a prison midwife support group to ensure that the specialist prison midwives that are in post are able to get together to share good practice and highlight any concerns. The group meet regularly.

Scans and specialist referrals are usually facilitated in the hospital nearest to the prison and women are usually accompanied by two prison officers (not necessarily female), unless they have been given permission for a hospital visit, released on temporary license (ROTL). The woman does not get a choice on which hospital she attends. Mothers are frequently handcuffed for these appointments (despite most being absolutely no flight risk at all). As highlighted in Chapter One, all women received into custody are (or are supposed to be) offered a pregnancy test. Several mothers in our research only found out they were pregnant on reception into prison, sometimes already in the second trimester, and thus having no previous antenatal care or notes. Tarian from Baldwin's research describes her shock at finding out she was pregnant on her reception into prison: "I had no idea I was pregnant, at first

I was dead worried ... thought I'd miscarry and everything ... the stress was awful."

Pause for thought

- Why might women not know they are pregnant until they are received into prison?
- Why might some women refuse the pregnancy test and what can this mean for them and their baby?
- How could this be addressed positively?

Pregnancy, prison and hospital appointments

In the community setting it is normal to have a named midwife for all pregnant women, and all women will be given a 24-hour number (sometimes the maternity ward as opposed to a direct line to the named midwife) to contact if they have serious concerns or worries. For most women in prison this is not possible. At HMP Low Newton mothers do now have 24-hour access to a midwife through a mobile phone with a pre-programmed number inputted, and it is hoped that this practice will be expanded to other prisons. Although some prisons, as previously mentioned, now do have a specialist midwife based in the prison when the authors undertook their research, many prisons did not.[2] In Abbott's research it was found that there was inconsistency in the three prisons where she undertook her ethnographic study. Alarmingly there was no cover organised for when the midwife went on annual leave in one of the prisons and when another midwife retired there was no replacement for her so women were often left without antenatal care or support, leaving a large gap in what is expected in the community for all women. During the COVID-19 pandemic women had even less access to support, especially as it was reported that women would be locked up in their rooms for 23 hours a day. Obstetric care is available for more complex and high-risk cases and always facilitated in the hospital, rather than the obstetrician visiting the woman in prison. In the latest report into the case of Ms A, the PPO suggested that without exception, all prison pregnancies should be treated and deemed as 'high risk'.

A concept borne from Abbott's research involves the experience of shame pregnant women prisoners go through when being taken from prison to hospital for scans and appointments. Using the phrase 'institutional ignominy' Abbott (2020) captures the concept and designates the pain of stigma moving from inside to outside of prison. Abbott's findings reveal that ignominy intensified as an institutional response to pregnancy as women felt 'paraded' in public while feeling 'branded' with prisoner emblems like handcuffs or even the prison officers and their uniforms themselves. The inner torment this caused the pregnant mothers was often expressed in indignation, sadness, shame and sometimes anger. The mothers felt that the presumed public opinion was that they were failing as a mother, were already bad mothers, and were dangerous, which the mothers felt was unwarranted. The term institutional ignominy captures the distinct experience of pregnancy in prison overall, unique among accounts of incarceration. As pregnant prisoners the mothers described feeling humiliation, demonisation and dehumanisation (Abbott et al, 2020). As articulated by Jade and Lola:

> Today they came for me to take me to a hospital appointment. I had no idea I had an appointment as the prison cannot tell me in case I decide to make a run for it! They took me in the long chains as apparently cuffs are no longer allowed now, I am 7 months [pregnant]. I walked into the antenatal clinic with the officers, them in full uniform, me looking a right mess as I did not even have time for a shower. All the other Mum's were staring at me in the waiting room – I was mortified! Me flanked by two officers, in chains looking like I must be a mass

murderer. I felt very much like crying but just kept my head down low. I felt physically sick with the shame of it. I feel like telling the whole waiting room that I am only on remand. I feel so ashamed and cannot wait to get out of there. (Jade in Abbott, 2018)

Similarly, Lola describes her internalised shame at being pregnant in prison and being escorted to hospital appointments: 'I'm handcuffed to an officer in prison uniform, and I'm pregnant and everybody is looking … and you can see people, they think "what has she done?" People shouldn't judge people; they should listen to your story first' (Lola in Abbott et al, 2020: 668). This was not an isolated incident, as Abbott found in her research:

I had my appointment in the hospital today. I am six months pregnant, but my clothes don't cover my bump, they're too tight. I had to go with two officers, and they put me in the chains because apparently they're not allowed to cuff me now, I am this big. The chains made it even more embarrassing as I had to walk through the main hospital. I have never felt so many eyes on me, staring like, making me feel like I'm a mass murderer – and I'm still on remand! I haven't even been convicted or sentenced yet. By the time I got to the clinic, and they took my blood pressure, it was through the roof. I tried to explain it was because I was stressed but they didn't listen to me. They spoke to the officers and not me. I wanted to ask some embarrassing questions about some discharge I've been having but I was too ashamed to ask in front of the male officers that know me from the wing. I was relieved to get back to the prison, I just sat and cried the total humiliation of it all. (Abbott, 2018)

Women in Abbott's (2018) research spoke of their frustration at the restraints being deemed necessary, highlighting their low level of risk and flight risk, their physical pregnancy size, and their own reluctance to do anything that might jeopardise their space on the MBU. It has not been normal practice for women to be in cuffs or in chains in birth since 1996, and according to Prison Service Instruction 33/2015 and the National Security Framework 6.20–6.32, 'restraints must not be used when attending medical appointments for this cohort unless there is a clear justification for doing so'. Furthermore, the directions are that 'if restraints are required, escort chains (long chains) must be used'. However, as was clear from our studies, the guidance was not always adhered to, and cuffs and chains were used regularly. Similarly, guidance issued to governors/directors via the *Pregnancy, Mother and Baby Units and Maternal Separation Policy* framework stipulates that 'wherever possible women should have confidential interactions with healthcare professionals, or to provide care to the baby where applicable'. However, again in our research, it was clear that the guidance was inconsistently applied.

Adapted from the new policy rules, a resource was developed by Abbott and the PMAG team to ensure guidance for officers escorting pregnant women was easy to access by developing it as a one-page sheet. It has since been agreed by HMPPS and shared across the female prison estate. This includes guidance on handcuffs and trauma-informed escort procedures, for example, officers to leave the room for intimate examinations, consultations, breastfeeding, and so on (Ministry of Justice and HMPPS, 2021).

Some mothers described officers refusing to leave during appointments, during scans, or officers only being behind a curtain while they were being intimately examined. Paige, in Baldwin's research, described having to breastfeed in front of officers and feeling very uncomfortable, especially while trying to get her baby to latch. Some mothers were so uncomfortable at the thought of 'having to feed' in front of officers that they chose to bottlefeed their newborns instead.

In both of our studies, there were some examples of excellent, caring and compassionate responses from prison staff to the pregnant and new mothers. Mothers reported that officers were sometimes 'lovely' and 'understanding', but also reported inconsistencies in care and, sadly, despite clear and specific guidelines these inconsistencies also related to antenatal care and food.

Pause for thought

- What do you think the perception of a member of the general public would be if they saw a pregnant woman in handcuffs at the hospital?
- What would your thoughts be?
- What would you imagine her crime was? (Over 80 per cent of women are imprisoned for nonviolent offences, like benefit fraud or shoplifting)
- Can you imagine what it feels like for the pregnant or new mum to be at hospital in cuffs or chains?

Pregnancy, prison and food

During pregnancy, energy requirements are increased and it is imperative that the diet provided meets nutritional recommendations, satisfies needs, and provides a healthy diet and lifestyle for pregnancy (Abbott, 2018). In Abbott's (2018) study the mothers' opinions of food provided varied considerably with the quality, inconsistency and resources resulting in a negative experience, highlighting the lack of stability across the prison system. The provision of starchy carbohydrates was a reoccurring theme which appeared within Abbott's research, often accompanied by comments relating to the 'stodginess' of them or the source of carbohydrates (for example, potatoes): 'the most processed food you can get, that is basically what it is. The potatoes are not potatoes, they are not real, they are like those smash things, the meat is the cheapest cuts you can get' (Pamela in Abbott and Tammam, 2019: 15).

Women reported that often the food was on a four-week rota which made the choices boring as well as undernourishing. Further, pregnant women experiencing normal physiological changes such as nausea and vomiting found the food system difficult and the diet unhealthy. Having an unhealthy diet was something else that added to the mothers' guilt about being pregnant in prison: 'The food here is disgusting – it is just stodge. I feel really unhealthy there is no fresh fruit no fresh vegetables. My midwife has told me that I need to eat more leafy green vegetables. It is impossible in here when all I get is potatoes' (Sharon in Abbott, 2018: 79). Several mothers in Abbott's research were concerned about nutrition and, worryingly, several lost weight. Although some of the mothers knew their entitlements in terms of extra food by way of a 'pregnancy pack', this still did not guarantee mothers received all they were entitled to:

> Well, apparently, you get two extra pillows, which I haven't got; you get extra milk, which I don't get; you get extra fruit, which I don't get; you get night snacks, which I don't get; and you get use of a toaster at dinnertime, which I don't get. So, loads of good things that you just don't get. (Jolene in Abbott, 2018: 84)

Michelle in Baldwin's research stated: 'One the things I remember most about being pregnant in prison was feeling hungry, *all* the time, I was hungry all the time' (Baldwin, 2021a: 172). Our findings echoed those of Smoyer and Lopes (Abbott, 2017: 240–255), who found that the inflexibility of routines also impacted on the women and their meals. Several women found that they felt so sick at certain times that they couldn't eat, but they had no choice and if they didn't eat when the meals were provided then they lost the opportunity to eat. Furthermore, mothers described having their evening meal at 5pm, with nothing further until 8am the next morning. This particularly impacted mothers who were low on funds and did not have the opportunity to buy 'canteen'.[3]

Following the formal *Review of Operational Policy on Pregnancy, Mother and Baby Units and Maternal Separation*, and the implementations of the PMBLOs, it is hoped that the basic needs of pregnant women in prison will be more likely to be met (Abbott, 2018, 2023). It is a travesty not to mention a health ticking time bomb for mothers and their babies, that mothers in prison were not/are not getting access to the nutrition that would not only keep them healthy, but that would facilitate the growth of a healthy baby. Pregnant mothers in our research, not least because unlike in the community mothers would have 24-hour access to maternity care and guidance, were often 'desperate' to attend their hospital appointments for reassurance that all was well. However, attending the hospital as an incarcerated women was not without issue.

Pause for thought
- Had you ever thought about pregnancy, prison and food before?
- Is additional food as a pregnant woman a right or a privilege?

Miscarriage and births in prison

Up until 2021, miscarriages and terminations in prison were not recorded and as such government understanding of the circumstances around these events is scarce. However, our research can provide some descriptions of women's experiences of miscarriage in prison. In Baldwin and Epstein's (2017) research, of three pregnant mothers, one stated that she had nothing but positive things to say about her treatment or about staff responses to her, but both of the other two mothers miscarried in prison and had mixed responses. Polly miscarried on the way to hospital 'in handcuffs', and describes her experience as follows:

I was pregnant and had had two episodes of spotting – which they knew, and they still put me on my own. I wanted to see a midwife and I was told I couldn't. I'd have to see the nurse. I was upset and wanted to ask loads of questions, but I never got to ask them because I lost the baby anyway. I think it was the shock of going to prison that made me lose my baby. I had no history of miscarriage, there was no other reason. When I lost my baby, I was bleeding on my own in my cell for hours. I was terrified, and the prison said they would get me to the doctors in the morning. I was in so much pain they called an ambulance eventually. I lost my baby on the way to the hospital, in handcuffs. I will never forgive them for that. There was no need for cuffs. I wasn't exactly running away, was I? (Polly in Baldwin and Epstein, 2017: 29)

Similarly Michelle also miscarried in prison, and she believes that her miscarriage was 'down to the stress of being locked up' (Baldwin and Epstein, 2017: 29), nonetheless Michelle had nothing but praise for how she was responded to and 'looked after' by prison staff both during and after her miscarriage. Anecdotally, as researchers we have heard many stories from mothers about their knowledge of mothers who have given birth or miscarried in prison and the responses we have heard about have ranged from compassionate, professional and competent to inadequate, cold, neglectful and dangerous. The inconsistency of care and responses is something the recent policy review hopes to address, but there is no doubt that experiencing pregnancy in prison is most often a worrying and troubling experience.

Several mothers described to us their very real fear of giving birth in prison, some mothers were aware of the recent deaths of babies previously born in prison or of other 'cell births' and this only served to exacerbate their fears. Abbott's (2018) research found that the sense of disempowerment at being left unsupported in labour, fear of not being unlocked in time for birth, and the lack of privacy was distressing for all mothers who laboured in prison, and this sometimes influenced a woman's choice in the mode of delivery of her baby, that is, some mothers requested an elective caesarean over a natural birth, just so that they could have some control:

> Sometimes the staff don't have the keys, so you've got to wait for someone … I don't want to be buzzing and buzzing people for them to get an ambulance, I just want them to book it [the caesarean]. It's all right anyway to get a caesarean now. It's my right if I ask for one. (Abi in Abbott, 2018: 109)

The sense of having no control over her pregnancy: where she would give birth; who might support her; receiving medications prescribed on the outside; and ultimately whether she would be allowed to remain with her baby beyond delivery, generated distress among all of the mothers in our studies. Abbott again quotes Abi who stated: 'I know people that have died in labour, I'm just scared of going in labour in here they just leave you' (Abi in Abbott, 2018: 87).

When a woman's labour begins in prison, either by her having regular contractions or if it is suspected that her membranes have spontaneously ruptured (waters breaking), she will usually be transferred to the local hospital in a taxi or prison van, again most often accompanied by, and handcuffed to, prison officers. In the UK it is a legal violation for anyone other than a registered midwife or medical practitioner to attend women in childbirth, except in 'sudden or urgent necessity' (Nursing and Midwifery Order, 2001), and yet Abbott found in her research that non-midwifery staff were making decisions as to whether women were in labour or not (despite the mothers themselves insisting that they were). Layla, a mother in Abbott's research, gave birth to her baby in her cell at 36 weeks. Her baby was presenting foot first, a risky presentation with a high risk of morbidity, and as such would normally require the presence of an obstetrician as well as a midwife. Layla had lost her mucous plug,[4] which in her previous labour had signalled her labour and imminent birth. Yet despite relaying this to healthcare, Layla was dismissed and locked up. Her repeated insistence that she was in labour was rejected by staff (non-midwives). Layla accepted her position of powerless prisoner, rather than labouring woman: ' "I'm telling you I am in labour," "No, you're not. Here's some paracetamol and a cup of tea"' (Abbott, 2018: 130).

Layla ultimately did give birth in her cell without a midwife present (nurses were in attendance but not midwives and one was male so was directed to wait outside the cell). Layla told Abbott that she was 'confused' and shocked by her birth experience, stating: 'I just want to know what happened.' No plans had been activated for a place on an MBU and therefore Layla was left not knowing whether or not she would be able to keep her baby: 'not knowing whether I would have to hand (baby) out or if she was coming back with me'. This lack of knowing meant that Layla did not know what she should do about feeding: 'To sit there not knowing whether to breastfeed or not breastfeed? Is she staying with me, she isn't staying with me?' The newborn baby was transferred with Layla from prison, via ambulance, to the local hospital but she had no provisions for the baby: 'I had nothing for her, no clothes, no nappies, because I was still in the main jail, and I wasn't allowed any baby stuff in. It was September – freezing – so I had to just wrap her up in clothes, completely naked underneath my nightie. She had nothing' (Abbott, 2018: 130–131).

In Baldwin's study the four mothers who gave birth during their prison sentence highlighted how important it was to them to have 'good' officers on duty when they were in labour, and how they hoped for a 'good' officer when they would eventually go to the hospital to give birth. This was best summed up by Kady:

You just prayed it wasn't one like Mrs White,[5] or the ones that ignored the bell, we all heard the horror stories of giving birth in a cell, one woman I know did and she nearly died, but the thought terrified me so, yeah, I wanted Mr Pink or Miss Blue, they always made me feel supported and didn't judge me … some of them others well they just make me feel shit as a Mother, man they really did … but Mr Pink and Miss Blue they used to even take the cuffs off me at the hospital scans … they were kind, man. (Kady in Baldwin, 2021a: 211)

Bozkurt's (2022) findings have echoed those of the authors, and Bozkurt describes the labour experience of a mother in her study:

I rang the bell, and they were taking ages to come … I explained look I'm having contractions … she said when your mucus shows, I want you to tell me. So I put a pad on and then when the show came I pressed the buzzer and eventually she came and … said where is it? you have to show me. I felt like a piece of shit. I had to take the pad out of my knickers and hold it up to the flap and then she said you'll have to wait; we don't have any staff. I was in pain, having contractions. I was so frightened. I was 19 and this was my first baby. Eventually, a nurse came and measured my contractions and said yeah you're in labour, but you'll be fine for now and she went off. I was in the cell all night. They left me there until the morning, in severe pain … I was handcuffed and taken to the hospital … the officers were in my labour. (Tanisha in Bozkurt, 2022: 101)

Tanisha's experience was 'horrific and degrading', especially in the final stages of her pregnancy. Bozkurt called leaving Tanisha her in a cell during the night an act of 'blatant disregard' (Tanisha in Bozkurt, 2022: 101). Unfortunately, Tanisha is not alone with this experience. As mentioned in Chapter One and revisited in more detail in the final chapter, in recent years two mothers have tragically given birth to stillborn babies, one mother in her cell overnight (Ms A) and the other mother in her cell toilet (Ms B, aka Louise Powell). A third baby was stillborn in an ambulance on the way to hospital. Thus it is plain that not all women are given timely or appropriate care, and as deaths of these three babies show all too painfully, the consequences of such failures can be devastating.

Following birth, dependent on whether a woman has been allocated a place on a prison MBU, she will return either to the MBU with her baby, or to the general prison without her baby.

Pause for thought

- How has it made you feel reading this section?
- Do you need to talk this through with someone?
- Were you aware of prison births and the baby deaths? If not, why do you think that is?
- What do you think the legacy of a prison birth might look like?

Mother and baby units

The application

MBUs house mothers who have given birth during their sentence, and mothers who were sentenced with age eligible children (under 18 months), who have made a successful application and been allocated a space. As discussed in Chapters One and Seven, the rejection rates for application the MBUs is varied, inconsistent between units, but overall can be low. For mothers refused a place they progress through their pregnancy knowing they will be separated from their babies a few hours after birth, something Abbott (2018: 157), calls 'the ultimate pain'. However, for mothers who know they will be separating from their babies at birth, the pain is long and slow, and the mothers feel it every day. Some mothers choose to try to 'disconnect' from their babies in this waiting period, while others, like Mary mentioned earlier, choose to savour every second their baby is with them (inside them).

> When they listen to his heartbeat, I feel like I don't want to get too attached, like a coping mechanism and then I feel guilty like 'how can you not want to be attached to your own child? I'll be crying my eyes out, thinking, 'I'm not going to know him' ... and then he'll start kicking and it's like he's saying, 'you do know me' ... and it's almost like he's saying, 'I'm here, I'm fine' ... I know they kick at random times, but, to me, it's like a sign, it feels like he is talking to me. (Caroline in Abbott et al, 2023a: np)

Abbott describes Lola's reaction when she heard the news she did not have her MBU space, 'all of them said no, and I just put my head in my jumper, and I wouldn't face them. It was horrible knowing that he's getting taken' (Lola in Abbott, 2018: 157). Similarly, another mother in Abbott's research described the impact of her impending separation, 'It's mainly when we're locked in when it (impending separation from baby) hits me the most ... I get panic attacks' (Abbott, 2018: 70). For some mothers, even if they were to secure an MBU space, separation would remain an inevitability (the upper age limit is 18 months – it will occasionally, and at the discretion of the governor, be extended to a maximum of two years). Celia spoke of her anxiety.

> I had to apply, and you could get turned down, so I'm thinking 'oh my god, I'm not going to get a place' ... all these things are going through my mind again the board ... were saying 'well because your sentence length is so long, you won't be able to keep the baby, you'll have to separate'. (Celia in Abbott and Lockwood, 2020: 56–57)

Abbott and Lockwood described how mothers waiting for their MBU decision or waiting for the separation 'down the line' felt like they were living on 'borrowed time' (Abbott and Lockwood, 2020: 56). The mothers in our research felt 'exhausted' by the fear of, and the reality of, impending separation (Abbott and Lockwood, 2020; Abbott, 2023). The death of Michelle Barnes (discussed further in Chapter Seven) all too painfully reminds us of the danger of separating mothers from their newborn babies, even if it is deemed to be in the 'best interests of the child' and believe to be an appropriate decision – that often doesn't make it any easier for the mother to bear. It is especially painful for mothers who have been seen to be pregnant on the wings, to return to the prison without their baby:

> Going back to the wing was like a walk of shame, my baby was gone, and I know the other mothers and especially the staff would have been thinking 'what did she do to risk losing her baby', they would have imagined it was something really bad. I felt embarrassed and ashamed … like the worst mother in the world. (Erin in Baldwin, 2022a: 170)

Not all mothers with eligible children will make an application to an MBU. This can be for a variety of reasons, including not wanting to attract attention and assessment from social services, not wanting to be so far away from home or, from Baldwin's (2022a) research, in Rita's case, because she had to make an awful choice, one in which she was the loser no matter what choice she made. Rita had four children, and when she was sent to prison (unexpectedly), she was initially sent to a prison relatively close to her home. However, she had a child eligible to come into prison with her, but the closest MBU would have been many miles from home. Meaning that Rita's other children would not be able to visit easily or frequently. As such, Rita made the unimaginable and heart-breaking decision not to apply for an MBU space and leave her baby at home. Doing so meant that all her children would 'stay together', and Rita would be able to see all of them regularly rather than just the baby all the time and her older children infrequently. Other mothers do not apply because they know that an application will trigger the involvement of social services for the assessment and if social services were not previously involved, some mothers wish to avoid this, for reasons outlined in Chapter Three. Not all mothers are eligible to apply because of their offences or their substance misuse status.

Echoing Sikand's (2015) research, both Baldwin and Abbott found that for some mothers finding out they had a space on the MBU came very late in their pregnancies, sometimes even after birth. Kady in Baldwin's research describes how she gave birth to her daughter 'not knowing if she would be taken' away and she would have to return to the prison without her. Fortunately for Kady the hospital midwives were sympathetic, and Kady remained in hospital until the decision was made and thankfully Kady was given her space. Not all women are informed in a timely manner that they can apply at all (although the new guidance should address this). For Beth, in Baldwin's research, no one told her she was eligible to apply for an MBU space, and when she did realise she was told it was 'too late' as she was serving only a four-month sentence. Beth describes her devastation at later finding out she could have brought in her solely breastfed baby: "[H]onestly, it broke me, I could have had her, I wouldn't have lost her, she would have known me … it killed me." Because she had no one in her family suitable to care for her baby Beth's baby girl was taken into care, and her social worker 'refused' to bring Beth's baby to the prison. As a result, when Beth returned home she felt her baby no longer knew her and Beth felt their bond was broken. This sent Beth on a downward spiral and, tragically, never recovering from her lost time with her daughter, Beth took her life a year after we had met. Her daughter remained in care, until her presumed adoption.

'Like living in a goldfish bowl'

Although all of the mothers in our research were glad and 'grateful' to be able to keep their babies with them, life on a prison MBU was not without issues. Abbott (2018: 100) suggests that the anxieties of being a new mother on an MBU are exacerbated by the milieu, the noises, atmosphere, postnatal emotions and having to cope with a new baby. This is compounded by the mothers' remoteness, of being away from family, and the impotence the new mothers felt in not being able to control their environment. Although MBUs are colourful, child-orientated, filled with baby paraphernalia and obviously have more comforts and freedom than the rest of the prison, mothers were very aware they were in a foreign, 'abnormal' environment. Mothers across our research described how they were 'made to feel grateful' that they had a space on the MBU, but felt their place was under threat of being removed and their baby 'sent out', at any point (Baldwin, 2022a). Kady describes what this was like for her:

> I remember they used to say all the time about being on the Unit 'it's a privilege not a right to be here', man they used to make threats all the time that our babies would be sent out – we had all heard stories of mothers this happened to, and one girl I was in with said it had happened when she first was on the Unit, they sent a baby out because the mum had answered back a few times so then she was a real goody two shoes after that cos she was scared. (Kady in Baldwin, 2022a: 169)

Abbott (2018) and (Baldwin, 2021a) found that staff relationships and how the staff were with mothers played a huge part in how settled the mothers felt and how positively (or not) the mothers experienced prison. Mothers in Baldwin's (2022a) study described the feeling of being 'surveilled' or 'watched' all the time, Kady described it as a 'goldfish bowl'

(Baldwin, 2021a: 205), Erin described feeling like staff 'were just waiting for us to fuck up so they could take our babies'.

Although some mothers described some staff as 'supportive' on the MBUs, there were also descriptions of judgmental staff who gave the impression to mothers that they didn't want to work on the unit, and fundamentally disagreed with babies being 'in prison' (the new guidance suggests that all MBU staff should have volunteered to work there and will have had appropriate and contextual training and knowledge). Abbott (2018) found that access to midwives was inconsistent during pregnancy and that remained the case in the immediate period following birth. As new mothers, especially those who were first-time mums, the bonding the mothers did on the unit with each other was important. Significant in both of our research was the support mothers felt they were able to gain from and give to each other. In the community, women can usually choose to access antenatal classes and groups like National Childbirth Trust classes. In prison there is inconsistency and many mothers' only support is each other. Many of the friendships mothers made on the unit have endured post-release (Abbott, 2018; Baldwin, 2022a).

Some charities, such as Birth Companions, run established pregnancy groups but they are currently only in a few prisons. Abbott's (2018) research findings highlighted the benefits felt by those who had accessed antenatal and postnatal/new mother classes run by the Birth Companions volunteers. Mothers found them, and the support they felt from each other, invaluable: 'It's not until you look back and see, the little groups were so important in there, just being able to talk to someone, just something little, you know, just like, how will I know I am in labour? Just to be able to ask someone that question' (Frances in Abbott, 2018: 107). The relationships with other mothers was important, because as Paige states, 'no one else understands what it feels like, or what we were going through'. Despite their gratitude for their space and the opportunity to stay with their babies, all of the mothers in Baldwin's research who spent time on an MBU also felt guilt about their babies 'living in a prison'. 'Yes you want to be on the MBU, you'd do anything to stay together, but that doesn't mean you like living with your baby in a prison, babies shouldn't see keys and uniforms and chains ... but they do here, that gets to you' (Carla in Baldwin, 2021a).

Bozkurt's (2022) recent research echoes this finding and she describes Sadia expressing similar feelings: 'I was so conflicted you know, am I a bad mum? Like I've got him in prison with me. Am I doing the right thing or is my breast milk not good enough because I'm stressed ... so many conflicting thoughts' (Bozkurt, 2022: 102). This guilt was exacerbated for the mothers every time they were 'reminded' they were 'still in a prison'. Kady describes how she felt following a cell spin:[6]

> [T]hey threw all her stuff man ... my baby's clothes everywhere. They took all my stuff down ... everything off the walls, they took my comfort didn't they? ... It was like ... remember where you are ... don't get too comfortable ... it wasn't the mother and baby unit no more ... It was just prison ... make no mistake it was prison. (Kady in Baldwin, 2018: 54)

'Food' reared its head again in the MBUs and was another issue that added to new mothers' guilt. Mothers described, again, not having the additional food by way of breastfeeding packs consistently delivered, which were an important source of the additional calories much needed by breastfeeding mothers. Some mothers who had allergies and could not have the nuts and fruit that come in the pack spoke of how their needs were not accommodated, they were simply told 'oh sorry' when they said they couldn't have the packs with nuts in. Other mothers spoke about the challenges of being able to make healthy and balanced meals for their babies when weaning. Paige described how she felt that "the support and guidance around cooking for your child is minimal. Women should be cooking sustainable foods for preparation of release and weaning etc but also for their health!'". Paige also described how there were strict rules about babies in the kitchen and so this meant that

> 'all of a sudden your child has to learn to occupy themselves while you cook a meal for them. ... One of the hardest things I found was listening to my daughter cry because she all of a sudden could not understand why my time was devoted to her during the hour I was cooking.' (Paige)

Bozkurt (2022) argues that minoritised women must deal with racism and prejudice on several levels, which she states may be both traumatising and harmful. Bozkurt goes on to say that the trauma caused by such experiences is rarely discussed or acknowledged, especially in relation to criminalised women (Bozkurt, 2022). In her research with ethnically minoritised criminalised mothers, Bozkurt heard testimony from mothers who felt their experiences in prison and on an MBU were affected by racism. Sadia felt that she and her son were treated differently on the MBU because of her ethnicity. She stated that her evidence was found in the fact that her son was not 'taken out' by nursery staff as much as the 'mum's gone to Oxford kinda kids'.

Mothers have described how 'cultural practices' (such as tightly wrapping their child or co-sleeping) have been interpreted differently because of institutionalised and personalised racism. The impact of being perceived to be acting in a 'negative' or 'risky' way on an MBU is potentially huge, and mothers can be perceived as being 'non-compliant', which may put their MBU place at risk (meaning mother and child may be separated). Mothers in our research described the threat of separation being used to secure compliance.

Nonetheless, mothers who did spend time on an MBU were usually positive about the experience. Tarian in Baldwin's (2022a) research felt that her bond with her baby, her youngest child of five, was the strongest of all of her children because of her time in an MBU. She states that having her son in the 'quiet' of the MBU as opposed to the 'noise and chaos' of her life before prison allowed her the time and space to 'be a real and present mother'. Ironically, the prison space had provided Tarian with a sanctuary from her home chaos and created a space where she could 'just be a mother' (Baldwin, 2022a: 137). This break from her pre-prison offending lifestyle cemented in Tarian the will and motivation to 'stay clean' when she left prison. Despite a long history of established 'drug dealing and wheeling and dealing', once she left prison Tarian remained determined to 'never be separated from' her children again and has not returned to prison or to her 'old lifestyle'. Paige sums up the complex emotions she felt as a mother on an MBU:

> 'My time on the unit had its journey of emotions, part of me felt guilt and a tremendous amount of shame for bringing her [daughter] with me to the prison, after all what kind of mother could do this? But the other half always reminded myself, actually a strong mother does this! Because not only was I in prison 11 days before I was due to give birth, I was a first time mum and had no idea how to be a mum yet, I was isolated from everyone who would have helped me. But I dedicated myself to learning, and giving my undivided attention to my daughter to make sure no matter what she felt the love that would help her thrive. This was not the end of our journey but the beginning. I read books on parenting, and I looked for guidance from the other mums. We did good, she thrived!' (Paige)

Conclusion

Despite the challenges of MBU living, and the fact that MBUs are still attached to prisons as opposed to in the community, mothers and babies still benefit enormously from the opportunity to stay together. MBUs can be supportive spaces and are often staffed by empathic, informed staff doing their best to support new mothers and their babies. It is better for babies' physical wellbeing, their long-term psychological health and of course their emotional wellbeing and development (Stewart, 2015) to remain with their mothers. It is also important to note that mothers who spend time on an MBU are much less likely to go on to reoffend (Mulligan, 2019).

Nonetheless, pregnancy in prison is hard, exhausting and stressful. The threat of impending separation or of the unknown is anxiety-producing and potentially harmful to mothers. Babies on an MBU are in a prison, thus despite the positives, would a better option not be for pregnant mothers not to be sentenced or remanded to prison in the first instance (unless in the most extreme of circumstances), and prison MBUs to be replaced with residential supportive provision in the community?

Pause for thought

- What are your thoughts about babies 'in prison'?
- Do you think it is better to separate a mother and baby and for a baby to live a more 'normal' life or do you think babies should stay with their mothers?
- What informs your ideas on this?
- What age do you think babies should be permitted to stay with their mothers until (some countries allow mother and children to remain together in prison until age ten [the children go out during the day]).

The following chapter will take up the narrative in terms of the legacy of prison as a pregnant or new mother and will focus on the mothers' experiences post-prison.

FIVE

The persisting pain of incarcerated pregnancy and new motherhood

'Everyone just expects you to be happy and put it all behind you, but it's not like that, how can you – I think of it every day still.'

Paige, 2023

Introduction

The 'pains of imprisonment' (Sykes, 2007 [1958]), and even gendered pains of imprisonment to an extent (Crewe et al, 2017), are recognised and familiar, however our research responded to gaps in knowledge around the maternal pains of imprisonment (Abbott, 2018; Baldwin, 2021a). The pains of maternal imprisonment are not left at the prison gates, for the mothers (and their children and babies), the legacy of maternal imprisonment endures (Eaton, 1993; Baldwin, 2017, 2020a, 2022a; Masson, 2019). This chapter examines this legacy. It reveals how the shame women felt in prison persists post-release. It reveals the multi-layered traumatic impact of imprisonment on the mothers and their families, and the importance of 'hope' in resilience.

Post-prison guilt, stigma and shame

Layered shame

Research with post-release women found that there were many challenges specifically related to motherhood in the immediate aftermath of prison, but also significantly, for many years, and sometimes intergenerationally (Baldwin, 2021a, 2022a). Although feeling stigmatised is a common feeling for many post-release prisoners (Goffman, 1963), for mothers it was often specifically related to their motherhood and was frequently related to a fear of negative evaluation by others (Liss et al, 2013; Baldwin, 2022a).

> I hate people knowing that I was pregnant both times I went to prison, it was bad enough being judged in court … I think, well everyone thinks, it's worse being in prison pregnant … so no I don't tell people if I can help it … it's just wrong, innit, and those that I do tell or have told, well they just look down their noses at you … it's like, 'how could you?'. You can see it in their eyes. It makes them question what kind of person you are. (Tamika in Baldwin, 2022a: 192)

> 'When I was pregnant the next time [post-release], I could see when the midwives looked in my notes about my previous pregnancy, you could see it come over their faces when they read, I'd been in prison pregnant, it made me feel ashamed all over again, I could literally see them judging me.' (Kady)

Many of the mothers in Baldwin and Abbott's research had experienced discrimination, stigma and judgement in their pre-prison lives as women, as working-class women, as Black women, as women affected by substances, but they found that continued and was exacerbated in their post-prison lives. As illustrated by Jaspreet's statement, often there was an intersectionality to the mothers' experiences, and they were deemed triply or even quadruply deviant (O'Malley, 2018; Baldwin, 2022a).

For the mothers in Bozkurt's (2022) research, their ethnicity and culture sometimes added a further layer of shame to their already challenged post-prison motherhood experience, which then added to the 'burden' the mothers carried post-prison. Chigwada-Bailey (2003) argues that, often, Asian women can face additional challenges post-release because they are perceived to have brought shame and dishonour to their family, as well as ruined their own and their family's reputation and honour. Understandably this can have a huge impact on self-esteem, social status, and familial and social ties. Illustrating Bozkurt's (2022) argument that ethnicity and culture can exacerbate the impact of women's experiences of the CJS and beyond, Jaspreet, who was forced to leave twin babies 'outside' when she was sentenced, found that her pain and feelings of loss continued post-release:

> 'My family obviously told me I brought shame on the family, I flip between being shunned by those who know [about prison] and lying to those who don't ... obviously, I did know it would be like this. My culture is very judgemental, especially to women. ... It's worse because I'm a mother ... even now my mother-in-law gets digs in all the time, she told my husband I was not 'morally capable' of guiding them [the children] now and bringing them up. I lost my profession, too, and that doesn't help me feel good about myself at all ... that I can't practice anymore, but it is as a mother I feel the most ashamed. For my husband it is both, but for my mother-in-law ... to her I am not fit to be a mother.' (Jaspreet)

Chigwada-Bailey (2003) states that minoritised women's stigma is exacerbated by the prejudice they face based on their ethnicity, gender and social class, compounded by their criminal record. She goes on to say that 'the stigma of imprisonment is much stronger for Black women than it is for people of other groups', stating that this can make it harder to secure support and thus may have an impact on reoffending (Chigwada–Bailey, 2003: 131).

Spoiled maternal identity

Most of the mothers in our research spoke of the loss of a 'good' maternal identity (Baldwin, 2017, 2022a; Abbott, 2018), simply because they had been to prison pregnant or as a new mother. Prison, in the mothers' eyes, was simply incompatible with 'being a good mother' (Baldwin, 2021a: 169), and as such their maternal identity was 'spoiled'. This feeling was compounded by the fact the mothers felt they were also perceived as such by others. Mothers often felt that this view was shared by members of the general public, family and sometimes the professionals they encountered in their journey. For the mothers, feelings of inferiority and shame were present even in the instances (which are the majority), where the mother's offence was nonviolent, or had in no way reflected her ability to love or mother her children (O'Malley, 2018). Again, not being able to identify themselves as 'good mothers' added to the guilt and shame the mothers already felt about going to prison in the first instance (Baldwin, 2022a). '[C]ould I do this, could I be a good role model to my daughter as a mother who'd been to prison? As a mother whose baby was born in prison' (Kady in Baldwin, 2022a: 193).

Mothers who had been pregnant in prison or who had given birth during their sentence and spent time on an MBU often described themselves and their pregnancy/birth experience as 'tainted'. As Paige told Baldwin, 'my first time giving birth will always feel tainted'. Kady added that, 'I'm tainted now ain't I? Forever … I'll always be that mum that went to jail. Every time I hear that song "Tainted Love" … I think that's me that is' (Kady in Baldwin, 2017: 6). For pregnant mothers in prison who were separated at birth from their children, the guilt was exacerbated and layered, particularly for those mothers for whom the separation would be permanent. Abbott et al (2023a) argue that such mothers are impacted in unique ways, different even to those mothers who are forcibly separated in the community, stating 'this type of complex loss also denies a woman her identity as a "mother"' (Abbott et al, 2023a: np).

Mary from Baldwin's (2022a) study, and who we have seen in other chapters, described her shame and guilt about the fact that her youngest son had been born while she was 'a prisoner' and removed from her care.

> When they [her sons] found me all those years later, knowing the social had told him he was born when I was in prison made me feel so ashamed, as if it wasn't bad enough he was taken ... but to know he was born to a *prisoner* ... it just made me feel dirty. (Mary in Baldwin, 2021a, emphasis in original)

The mothers in our studies who had experienced babies removed from their care were painfully aware that any future pregnancy would also be subject to child protection procedures; thus even their '*future motherhood* continued to be stigmatised by the past' (Morriss, 2018: 823, emphasis in original).

Guilt

The repercussions of being a prisoner when pregnant go way beyond the prison gates, leaving the post-release mothers with painful feelings of guilt. Some women described how guilt manifested itself in many different ways and affected their mothering and mothering practices. For some mothers, after being released from prison, this impacted their levels of anxiety, often including a need for excessive cleanliness and a sense of not letting their child out of their sight (Abbott,

2018). Mothers in both Abbott and Baldwin's research spoke of the need to 'make it up' (Kady) to their children and babies that they had had 'that start in life' (Rita), either as an unborn baby in prison or as a baby on an MBU or a baby 'left outside' (Nicola). Other mothers in our research spoke of never wanting to discipline their babies and children, again as a means of 'making up' to them. Tanisha, whose baby was born during her prison sentence, described the post-prison guilt as having 'no end' (Baldwin, 2021a: 243).

Baldwin found that mothers often had an irrationality fed by guilt, with one mother even believing that her child's cancer had been caused by the stress of their separation (Maggie). Mothers told how if their children demonstrated any differences or weaknesses, delays in development, anything slightly out of the ordinary at all, they questioned whether it 'was because I went to prison' (Rita in Baldwin 2021a: 241). Beth's shame and guilt were layered: not only did she feel stigmatised as an ex-prison mother, but she worried about what her daughter would 'think of her' in the future when she found out she had been in care as a baby during her mother's prison sentence. Worrying about this fuelled Beth's lack of hope and her uncertainty about what kind of future they 'could have':

> The bairn had to stop breast feeding cos I was sent down … that's sick isn't it? Her health for life affected because of me and my mistakes. I felt like a shit mother, the worst in fact … she went into care because of me, I felt like nothing when I was in prison. … Even now I think what's the point of me. She doesn't know me now … I try in the contacts[1] like, but she doesn't want me … when I come out of my contacts, all I want to do is block out the pain with drugs … that or leave this life altogether … sometimes both. (Beth in Baldwin, 2022a: 195)

Baldwin's (2022a) research with post-release mothers found that mothers would experience feelings of guilt and shame for many years post-release and, for some, just as they felt it was lessening it would rear its head again many years down the line. Some of the mothers in Baldwin's (2021a, 2022a), research described experiences which were decades post-release, but the guilt and shame they felt at having experienced prison as a pregnant or new mother weighed on them heavily, and sometimes 'forced' the mothers to lie to their families – which served only to compound their shame. Margaret spoke of her ongoing guilt as a mother and grandmother. Margaret, already ashamed of ever having been in prison, had an additional 'secret', she had been pregnant in prison and her baby was taken into care and adopted. Margaret called her prison sentence and the prison birth of her baby 'a dirty secret', so 'ashamed' was she about her ex-prisoner status that she rarely even used the word 'prison', instead preferring to refer to it as when she was 'away':

> There are so many situations where I have to tell white lies to cover up for that period I was away. Just the other day my granddaughter asked me what I did for my 21st, well it was a kick to the stomach because I was away for my 21st. I just feel so guilty for lying but I'm too ashamed for them to know. ... I have to deny that first pregnancy, my firstborn baby, I deny his existence so that my children and grandchildren don't know I was a prisoner and a pregnant one at that. (Margaret in Baldwin, 2021a: 246)

Birth and starting life in prison

As mothers, most of us tell our 'birth stories', whether they are good or bad, many times in our lives. As mothers (of three children each and several miscarriages), we the authors have had both difficult and easy births with our children, but we have told them easily and readily, as most of us do. It is a rite of passage, sometimes a means of healing, often as a way of bonding with other mothers. However, for mothers who have given birth during a prison sentence, their birth stories are harder to share, not least because they most often have some unique and uncomfortable aspects to them. Mothers have described feeling guilty and ashamed about the fact they were prisoners when their babies were born and as result don't like to share their 'birth story', sometimes actively avoiding telling it. Paige gave birth with officers in the room and as such her 'birth story' is tinged with sadness, shame, guilt and regret:

> '[D]uring my time contracting, I had two officers at all times in the room. As I was pushing they allowed him [partner] in, I birthed our little girl and during what should be our most precious time I felt self-conscious, observed and uneasy. I wanted to breastfeed and felt judged for not knowing how to straight away, asking for privacy behind a curtain while I tried to feed her. Our journey was finished before we left the hospital because nothing felt natural. If I knew my rights from the beginning I would have asked them to sit outside my room and not at the bottom of the hospital bed.' (Paige)

Paige goes on to say how her partner was only allowed in during the very final stages (pushing stage). They were not allowed any communication at all during the rest of her labour, which Paige feels "spoiled it for him too", and which adds to her guilt.

Several mothers in Baldwin's research have spoken about their 'shame' that their child spent the first months of their lives on an MBU. Kady and Paige describe how their shame eats away at them and they are 'scared' to tell their children their history. Kady's daughter is almost a teenager now and Kady is yet to tell her daughter her birth story or the fact that she spent the first five months of her life in a prison MBU. Kady stated she had 'put off' telling her daughter 'because I feel like … like there's something just so wicked about it'. She is afraid of her daughter's rejection but also fears the reactions of others towards her daughter, worrying others would judge and negatively label her daughter a 'prison baby'. Kady still worries that her daughter won't 'forgive' her:

> I put her there, she didn't ask to be there. I just don't think she will [forgive], and the thing is I wouldn't even blame her if she hates me … but she will always be that child who was born in prison. My shame is her shame, or it will be when she knows, I don't want her tainted like me, why would I want her to know that about herself, about me, she's got the most horrible birth story forever, I did that to her, me. (Kady in Baldwin, 2022a: 193)

Similarly, although not so long after prison, Paige is already worrying about when the time comes to explain to her daughter her start in life.

> 'It's a conflicting battle on whether I will tell my daughter about her early months of life on the mother and baby unit. I still carry a lot of shame and guilt that this was her beginning of life and feel she will have always deserved better than what she was given. … It worries me how she would react, would she carry that burden? Or feel shame that she was born in prison? But I hope my years with her from now will instil good insight to actions and consequences. But as a mum I will always carry this with heavy shoulders.' (Paige)

For mothers who have actually given birth in the prison itself, any guilt and shame they may have felt is often overwhelmed by trauma and will be revisited in a later section.

Pause for thought

- Would you find it hard to tell people if you had received a prison sentence? If so, why?
- Would it be harder to tell people you have given birth in a prison or while serving a sentence? Why?
- What would your honest thoughts be if someone told you they had been pregnant/given birth in prison?
- Has hearing some of the mothers' stories made you think differently about pregnancy and prison?

The multi-layered legacy of prison pregnancy and new motherhood

'Inability to move on' and friendship

As Paige states at the outset of the chapter, mothers who have lived on an MBU are expected to simply 'move on' and 'be happy' that they are now free and can live a 'normal' life. However, as the mothers here will illustrate, it is not quite as simple as that. Mothers in Baldwin's research who had spent time on an MBU felt under pressure to put the experience 'behind them', to 'get on with it' and focus on their post-release present. However, none of the mothers found it easy. Abbott (2018) had highlighted how important these friendships had been as pregnant mothers in prison sharing the same experience. Mothers in Abbott's research spoke about how in other circumstances the women would be unlikely to become friends due to their differencing social circumstances, but in prison and post-prison they were 'best friends now' because of their shared experiences. Similarly, mothers in Baldwin's (2022a) study described how the support the mothers gave to each other was 'lifesaving' at times, because 'only they could understand' what each was going through.

This feeling of needing their emotions and experiences understood by those who had shared it in prison continued post-release and is the main reason many of the 'MBU mums' in our research have kept in touch. Indeed, the mothers who have co-written the following chapter in this book are part of a 'lived experience team' (hosted by Birth Companions). A group of over 40 women who have the shared experience of prison and/or MBU living as pregnant or new mothers. The very existence of this team and the wide geographical area the women are from highlights powerfully women's needs to maintain those bonds and feel understood and heard in a 'safe space'. Paige calls her relationship with her fellow MBU friends an "undeniable bond". Similarly, Jane from Abbott's (2018) research describes her bond with a fellow prison mother:

> 'It's funny, me and my friend Jem are still best friends, she is not from a rough background, she's been brought up well, she's been to Uni, she's a nice girl, we were probably the least bad girls you would ever meet in your life. Both of us and she's my best friend now. We've both been through that together with our babies.' (Jane, 2018)

Disrupted realities

However, the lifelong friendships the women sometimes make on an MBU do not come without cost. Several mothers in Abbott's (2018) research described mixed emotions and experiences of their life on an MBU. For mothers who lived in an MBU during the COVID-19 pandemic there are long-term impacts and consequences concerning relationships that are unique to the time. Despite a recommendation that pregnant mothers and mothers who did not pose a 'high risk'[2] and their babies should be released, in reality very few pregnant or new mothers were released, and with charities and third sector agencies being unable to access the prison estate, much of the face-to-face support was withdrawn from the women (Abbott, 2023). However, support did continue in a virtual way, and this was valued by pregnant women (Abbott, 2023). Nonetheless, some babies did not physically meet their father, their siblings, their grandparents and extended family for over a year after their birth. Babies were not taken outside to experience the outside world as they usually are from an MBU. Mothers have described to us the challenges their babies and families have faced post-release. Paige, who spent 11 months on the MBU with her daughter, all during the COVID-19 pandemic, states:

'My daughter still struggles with groups of people, and we have a big family who sometimes forgets this was not her everyday environment from birth. I have to try and explain to people that she just needs a bit of time – but even having to do that, well it just takes you back all the time.' (Paige)

Another mother, Sam, told us her child was terrified when she first took him out in the pushchair, he was scared of the traffic and found all of the sights and sounds of 'outside' overwhelming. It is important to remember that the impact of being on an MBU has an impact on the babies and toddlers too. Paige told us:

'Babies have so much to adapt to in any normal life circumstances outside, they soak everything up like sponges, and when you're released for ROTL or permanently it can be a shock to be surrounded by different visuals/sounds than their "normal" it is imperative they are able to socialise in public with everyday sounds, crowds of people and sceneries beyond those unit walls. Babies should not be conditioned to solely to the unit's environment it does have a long-lasting affect some more than others.' (Paige)

While lifelong friendships were formed on the MBU, it also had its downsides, as some mothers experienced factionalism, leading to isolation and exclusion. This has resulted in some mothers becoming suspicious of others and choosing to keep to themselves after their release, depriving themselves of crucial support, particularly for first-time mothers.

Finding resilience

The innate resilience and inner strength of the mothers in our research was a common thread through all the interviews, whether reflecting on a past prison experience or if currently pregnant in prison. In Abbott's (2018) research, the support of family outside, and even thinking of deceased family members as protective 'angels' were ways of coping for some pregnant women. Trixie's mother had died suddenly when she was a child, and she would talk about how she believed her mum was with her in a spiritual sense. At each interview, she would bring a photograph of her mother with her to share:

> I feel I'm strong, because I just keep my mum close to my heart. ... I'm going to make her proud by getting through it. ... It's not about trying to like act strong, it's when you are strong you like to just not think you're that strong, and just get on with it. Because then, when I'm at a good place, and I can look back, I'll know how strong I've been. (Trixie in Abbott, 2018: 142)

For others in Abbott's study, prison was just another challenging experience in a life full of complexity. An intangible force inside her kept Tammie going while pregnant: 'I don't know, it's just within. Sometimes I feel like, oh, I can't take any more, but I have to just keep going, innit?' (Tammie in Abbott, 2018: 143). Most women did just that and 'kept going'. The mothers did the very best they could to survive, but sadly, as we have seen, not all of the mothers made it – but we know they fought hard to try. Demonstrations of personal resilience and strength are not unique to pregnant prisoners, yet their type of pain required a special type of survival and strength. The sensations of their babies' movements were often helpful prompts that enabled women to harness an inner resilience while pregnant. The experience of the baby's movements and the privacy of that experience encapsulated the woman and her unborn baby together in a moment of pleasure and protection, cocooned in a world of their own that nobody could penetrate (Abbott, 2018). The unborn baby was a focus of resilience and strength and survival, allowing the mothers to take pleasure in the mother state, even if just transitorily.

Hiding vulnerability and weakness is a common experience for women in prison (Carlen and Worrall, 2004). Yet, for the pregnant woman, the increasing visibility of their pregnancy, coupled with an internal voice of having to stay strong for their unborn, sometimes meant internal struggles. The resilience demonstrated by most women in our studies shows the unique pains of a pregnant woman adapting to, and coping with, the prison environment. It appeared that trying to keep positive could only stretch so far as a coping mechanism for some of the mothers, especially those separated from their babies. Being outside of normal human experience, the enforced separation of a baby makes coping with imprisonment for the pregnant woman exceptional and outside the experience of any other person (Abbott et al, 2023a). Mothers in Abbott's research described how when in prison, distraction helped them to build resilience, and some found exercise, productivity or religion useful. Some mothers would say they 'just had to get on with it for the kids' (Abbott, 2018: 142). 'Throughout my whole life I've had struggles, and I've had to survive, I've been on my own since 16, and I've lived on my own, so I've seen a lot and had to go through a lot, so this is just another thing that I've had to go through' (Tammie in Abbott, 2018: 143).

This sense of 'just having to get on with it' persisted post-release, and mothers in Baldwin's (2021a) research would describe the same attitudes and distractions as being useful for building resilience. Baldwin argues that '[s]upporting and facilitating resilience should facilitate learning, understanding, coping and action' (Baldwin, 2023: 247). Baldwin remarked that 'hope' was an important part of resilience for the mothers in her study, and further noted in her research that guilt was a life-threatening emotion, and that hope often provided an 'an antidote to guilt' (Baldwin, 2022a: 129). Mothers *hoped* for a better future, *hoped* to be reunited with their babies and children, *hoped* that at least their removed babies would have wonderful lives, *hoped* they would be able to move forwards and heal. Despite facing an uncertain future, imagining and planning (Warr, 2016) for their maternal future was an important part of the mother's resilience. However, an important part of fostering and maintaining resilience was faith in the system, finding support and, more than that, finding support at appropriate and opportune times – when this didn't occur, that is when mothers lost hope. When they lost hope they lost motivation, and as the model shows in Chapter Three this was not infrequently when mothers had lost their children. Motherhood, if it is supported, can be part of a positive motivation to desist, to recover, to survive. However as demonstrated by Beth and Michelle Barnes, if motherhood and maternal emotions and maternal trauma are not supported, then resilience is much harder to achieve or maintain.

Mothers again identified the importance of supportive others. Post-release mothers frequently mentioned the lack of support they received from criminal justice professionals concerning their motherhood, and many felt that if they had been supported in their motherhood they would have felt more resilient. There is growing evidence to show an increase in mental ill-health in all women separated from babies (Abbott et al, 2023a). Abbott et al (2023a) found that mothers separated from their babies at birth during their sentence unsurprisingly suffered from feelings of loss and grief, and for those whose babies would not be returned to them, these feelings persisted post-release, making it hard to find resilience post-release. A woman's sense of failure at 'motherhood', following compulsory removal of a baby, reinforces feelings of shame and guilt Abbott, 2018; Broadhurst and Mason, 2020; Baldwin,

2022b). As Beth's tragic story illustrates, mothers who were unsupported in that loss and its impact remain vulnerable and at risk. For Beth, she was all out of resilience and could not come to terms with her lost bond with her daughter. Abbott et al (2023a) highlight the need for therapeutic and compassionate, informed responses to maternal loss while the mothers are still in prison, and Baldwin (2022a) highlights the importance of such support post-prison. Had either, or both, been available to Beth she may have found the strength to stay alive and her daughter would be with her mother. However, mothers in our research told us that they did sometimes find it hard to engage with or trust professionals post-prison.

Support: fear of asking/lack of

Mothers' reluctance to seek support was mainly because the mothers felt they would be judged more harshly because they had been to prison while pregnant or as a new mother, but also because of the 'ultimate fear' of losing their children (Baldwin, 2022a):

> If I said I was finding it tough, I knew they'd assume I was back on the drink, then they'd be all over me like a rash. I would have lost my kids forever this time … so I just kept quiet and managed … it nearly killed me, but I managed. (Shanice in Baldwin, 2021a: 252)

For the post-prison mothers, feeling unable to ask for help if they were struggling (again thinking back to the model in Chapter Three), meant that for some mothers further intervention came at a crisis point. This in turn created a situation where mothers were then more likely to have a(nother) child removed from their care or be in contact with the CJS, or re-imprisoned. Not wanting to 'risk' asking for help as an 'ex prison mother' was something several mothers in Baldwin's research mentioned, and this impacted the mothers in many different ways. Kady, whose first daughter had been born during her sentence, became pregnant again about eight years post-release. Kady struggled with her second pregnancy and baby and 'missed' the support of the MBU. But Kady described being afraid to ask for help, or mention this to the health visitor, because she thought she would be deemed 'incapable'. Kady struggled as a result and barely managed to 'stay out of trouble', falling instead into a deep depression as a result. Kady narrowly missed a second 'crisis point' and potentially a return to prison.

Mary (introduced in earlier chapters) was pregnant on reception into prison, her baby who was born during her sentence and was taken immediately into care at birth. In her chapter co-written with one of the book authors (Baldwin et al, 2022a), Mary describes her agony at being parted from her baby. She had waited until he was sleeping to allow the social workers to take him 'then, when he was sleeping, so he wouldn't know, I let them take him'. Mary describes how she was returned to prison a few hours after her son's birth, and 'thankfully' for her she was returned to the cell with her cell mate. Mary describes how her cell mate had secured some drugs for her in anticipation of her return. Mary had stated that as she had now lost both of her children, she did not know how else to cope with her 'shitty life'.

> Thank god I wasn't alone; I had a pad mate … or I don't think I'd be here now. She knew how I'd be feeling god bless her and she had got 'gear'[3] ready for me to take, that probably sounds weird and sick, but it was the most caring thing she could have done. I took it gratefully. (Mary in Baldwin et al, 2022a: 107–132)

In the absence of formal support, Mary sought solace in one of the very things that would trigger a further CJS response. Mary's response to the loss of her child illustrates Baldwin's circular 'missed opportunities' model (see Chapter Three), and further highlights the importance of supporting mothers in the post–removal/separation period (Barnes, 2015; Morriss, 2018; Baldwin et al, 2022a): 'So that was it, I got out eventually, no money, no home, no job and no kids. What was even the point in trying to stay sober' (Mary in Baldwin et al, 2022a: 116).

After losing her sons, Mary's downward spiral continued unsupported for many years. It was many years later that an enlightened prison officer asked Mary (about her children), 'If they come to find you what kind of Mary do you want them to find?' (Baldwin et al, 2022a: 116). Mary describes how this simple question triggered the motivation to address her unresolved trauma and subsequent substance use. Her intention became to 'get clean' so that if and when her sons came to find her, she could face them knowing she had 'got better' (Mary in Baldwin et al, 2022a: 117–132). However, highlighting the long-term and sometimes intergenerational impact of an incarcerated pregnancy and separation, tragically, Mary's sons had not been happily adopted as she had hoped. Instead, they had experienced many unsuccessful foster homes. They themselves had become 'career criminals' and in turn their children were affected by prison absences and damaged parents.

Difficult choices, difficult consequences

There are so many facets and relationships affected by incarcerating mothers. Rita, from Baldwin's study (2021a), as mentioned earlier, had made the difficult choice to leave her MBU-eligible toddler at home during her sentence. Rita's older daughter had taken on the care of her toddler sibling when her mother went to prison. Rita described how when she came home, her son, now aged three-and-a-half, would still look to his sister for his care needs to be met. Rita described a 'tug of war' over the child but acknowledged that her daughter now knew her son's needs better than she did. Rita said, 'she knew his favourite food, his favourite bedtime story, his best friends at nursery'. Rita went on to say that she was torn between feeling 'invisible', wanting to retreat further into the background of her family, or 'fighting' to regain her role and status as mother. Rita described how she had to renegotiate her relationships with all of her children and acknowledged that it took time for her to recognise they had all matured while she had been in prison and that a 'period of adjustment' was much needed (Baldwin, 2021a: 194).

Tarian, a mother of five, described how after her stay on an MBU, she was 'much closer' to her baby son, (her youngest of four) because while on the MBU, she was mothering in less chaotic circumstances than she had mothered her other children. Although for her and her baby this was a positive, this caused some resentment and challenges in her other children and affected Tarian's relationships with them post-release, again taking time to resolve.

It is clear from the snapshots and excerpts from mothers' narratives that prison as a pregnant and/or new mother can and does have long-lasting, sometimes lifelong, impact. The impacts run deep and affect multiple relationships in many ways. Some mothers benefit positively from the experience of an MBU but most of the mothers in our studies felt it was not without cost. A word that came up time and time again from our mothers was 'traumatic'.

Post-prison trauma

Although much is spoken about in terms of the trauma women take with them into prison, until Baldwin's research, not much had been written about the trauma women leave prison with, and even less specifically about the *maternal trauma* they leave prison with (Baldwin, 2021a, 2022a). Baldwin found that mothers' description of their maternal trauma post-release was often symptomatic of post-traumatic stress disorder (PTSD). For all of the mothers in these studies the impact of maternal imprisonment was felt far beyond their period of custody; the pain, the guilt and the shame they felt as mothers who did not 'live up' to ideals of motherhood and mothering contributed to their spoiled, and traumatised, maternal identities. Dee (a mother of four) eloquently describes what this felt like to her:

> The effects of that place haunt me, the physical scars on my arms only remind me of the pain and heartache I felt when I was in there. Just not being with my kids, man ... but worse for me are the mental scars that no one sees, everyone thinks I'm over it ... no one knows, but I'm wrecked really. I still have nightmares from that place you know. I'll always be that terrible mother that went to prison ... nothing will take that away. (Dee in Baldwin, 2018: 55)

Lauren's daughter was just under two years old when Lauren was sentenced to custody for her first offence. Her daughter was taken into care, but they were eventually reunited after Lauren's release. Here Lauren describes not only her own trauma, but her child's:

> [Y]es she hates being away from me ... she cries if I leave her, and I know that's because of what happened ... seeing her traumatised reminds me so much of how traumatised I felt in prison being away from her ... we need to get past it, we both do but it still feels so raw. (Baldwin, 2022a: 249)

Beth, the youngest mother in Baldwin's study, had predicted in her research interview that a return to drug use or suicide would be likely for her because of her struggle with guilt, shame and sadness at being sentenced to imprisonment as a new mother. Before her death, Beth's shame and guilt were layered with feelings of trauma. Not only did Beth feel stigmatised as an ex-prison mother, but she worried about what her daughter would 'think of her' in the future when she found out she had been in care as result of her mother's imprisonment. Worrying about this fuelled Beth's lack of hope and her uncertainty about what kind of future they 'could have' (Warr, 2016):

> The bairn had to stop breast feeding cos I was sent down ... that's sick isn't it? Her health for life affected because of me and my mistakes. I felt like a shit mother, the worst in fact ... she went into care because of me, I felt like nothing when I was in prison. ... Even now I think what's the point of me. She doesn't know me now ... I try in the contacts like, but she doesn't want me ... when I come out of my contacts, all I want to do is block out the pain with drugs ... that or leave this life altogether ... sometimes both. (Beth in Baldwin, 2022a: 195)

Baldwin has called guilt a 'life threatening emotion' (Baldwin, 2022a: 268), and tragically for Beth this proved to be true. Beth was so utterly traumatised by the enforced separation from her baby (who was three months old when Beth was sentenced), which, alongside her own negative self-evaluation of herself as a mother, proved too much for Beth to bear and Beth took her own life not much more than a year after her release from prison.

The legacy of a prison pregnancy or a postnatal, or MBU, separation on the mothers is profound and long-lasting. Again synonymous with symptoms of PTSD, some post-release mothers described 'flashbacks', 'recurrent nightmares' and 'bursts of anger'. For the mothers who gave birth in prison, or during their sentence, the mothers' trauma at their memories was often palpable. Louise Powell (Ms B), whose baby was stillborn in her prison cell toilet, has told us she 're-lives' her daughter's birth almost every night, often waking up crying at 3am. Louise is devastated at the loss of her daughter and traumatised by the circumstances of her birth. Louise has also spoken to us about her pain as a mother who feels her daughter was "let down" by the system and the prison itself. Louise tells us, that her pain is made worse and harder to bear because she feels she is "continuing to fight for justice".[4] Something she feels has been resisted and is very slow to come. Louise hopes that by waiving her anonymity and highlighting what happened to her and her daughter, Brooke-Leigh, she can "help other mothers avoid what I have had to go through". Louise and Ms A, whose baby was also stillborn in prison, are unlikely ever to fully recover from the trauma of their babies' births, births that should never have occurred in prison.

Tanisha spoke of her trauma at giving birth in prison, and for some of the mothers these traumatic memories were part of what trapped mothers in the cycles of substance misuse and reimprisonment.

> [H]onestly, I was mentally scarred by having Dwayne in prison ... I used to obsess over it. It was stupid but I couldn't put it behind me ... so I drank to cope but that just made things worser and I ended up back in again ... its crazy, I know ... it doesn't make sense, but it was all part of the same thing. (Tanisha in Baldwin, 2022a: 248)

Kady described how she often has nightmares from aspects of her imprisonment and feels that her anger issues are a symptom of her trauma and of not 'being able to process the memories of that place'. She describes how she was 'made' to return to 'education' in the prison when her baby was very young:

> They made me leave her at six weeks ... six weeks, man! ... and go to education, I had to listen to her screaming and not be able to go to her, how fucked up is that? I can feel myself getting angry thinking about it all now, it doesn't need to be like that. I mean why was it essential I go to a classroom and colour in! That's I was doing you know. (Kady in Baldwin, 2022a: 248)[5]

Emma, in Baldwin's (2021a) study, had served several prison sentences, two of them while pregnant. Her first daughter was taken into care during her previous sentence, eventually moving to live with her father. Highlighting the significance of supporting mothers in their maternal trauma (see the model in Chapter Three), Emma spoke of how she had 'spiralled out of control' after the trauma and loss of her first daughter. Emma found out she was pregnant again on her reception into prison for her penultimate sentence. She was released seven days before the birth of her daughter and hoped to be able to keep her child. Emma described how she was utterly traumatised by the memory of her daughter being unexpectedly taken into care:

> The memory of them coming into hospital with the car seat ... I had thought I was taking her home, but as soon as I saw the car seat I knew they were taking her. I remember hearing someone screaming and screaming and then I realised it was me screaming. I discharged myself and went and got off my face. I didn't know what else to do. (Emma in Baldwin, 2022a: 226)

Emma remained on that trajectory for some time, she says she asked repeatedly for support but wasn't heard or understood and Emma soon returned to prison. Tragically, Emma, who had previously said she felt like she 'had nothing else to live for', died five weeks after her release from prison from pneumonia. During her last sentence she had spoken about her losses and Emma had engaged with support in prison, and at the time of her death Emma was drug-free. Moreover, Emma had stated she was 'determined' and motivated to 'stay clean', primarily because she was 'desperate' to try to regain some contact with her first daughter.

Vicarious trauma

Vicarious trauma is another form of trauma experienced by women in prison, as Louise shared her own experience of her friends, particularly her cell mate, witnessing her stillbirth and being deeply affected by it, highlighting the significant emotional impact of witnessing such events and carrying those memories for years, as described by mothers like Paige witnessing the final contact and removal of a baby from the MBU:

'One mum had to have her baby taken out once she was sentenced and that separation wasn't handled very sensitively – we were all in the TV room when the social worker came to take the baby away and we all witnessed that baby being removed – that was distressing and insensitive. No one wants to see someone's child being removed – also, how can we comfort someone when we have our baby in our arms.' (Paige)

Mothers on an MBU can be separated from their baby for a number of reasons:

- because mothers had previously been remanded but have now been sentenced and as such the mothers' sentence may exceed the eligible age of an MBU stay for a baby (18 months);
- a baby may have reached 18 months or two years and is no longer eligible to stay on the unit but the mother may have time left to serve (governors can extend from 18 months to two years at their discretion);
- risks to the health and welfare of mother and/or baby are assessed to warrant separation;
- mother's own choice;
- babies should not be removed as a punishment for mother's 'behaviour' in prison but will be removed if mum has been found to be using drugs in prison.

Whatever the reason for a separation on an MBU, it will be painful for the mother, for the baby and for the staff. Grace tries to put into words how separating from her 19-month-old son felt when he went 'outside' to grandma (she had 12 months left to serve).

> 'The weeks before he was going out I could do nothing but cry, I felt guilty he was going out, guilty I'd kept him with me and now he had to go through this. ... I kept thinking how will he cope without me, how will I cope without him ... I felt like my heart was being ripped out. I will never ever get over it.' (Grace)

There is increasing evidence to show an increase in mental ill-health in all women separated from babies (Powell et al, 2017; Abbott et al, 2023a). For imprisoned women separating from their babies may exacerbate risk of self-harm and suicide. The suicide of Michelle Barnes in 2016 (see Chapter One) highlighted the psychological harm such separations cause and the need for developing and strengthening meaningful support in every prison. There are many aspects of prison as a pregnant and new mother that are incredibly painful. In many ways it is a wonder that more women are not lost. Maternal trauma is a risk factor in terms of suicide or self-harm (Baldwin, 2021a, 2022a), and it is a credit to the mothers' resilience that they get through it all.

Motherhood and desistance

Several mothers spoke to us about how new motherhood or having a child removed interacted with their desistance, and as the model in Chapter Three highlights, supporting mothers at these key moments in time is imperative, whether they are in prison or in the community (Baldwin, 2022a). Bachman et al (2016) have argued that while obviously motherhood in and of itself does not always inhibit offending behaviour (as this prosocial role did not prevent criminalised mothers from offending in the first instance), they argue instead that 'when offenders are ready to adopt a prosocial identity, reclaiming their role as mother may indeed serve to solidify their desired change' (Bachman et al, 2016: 215). Emma, and the other mothers here, powerfully demonstrated the need to factor in 'maternal trauma', 'motherhood and maternal emotions' in all trauma-informed approaches with women in contact with the CJS (Baldwin, 2022a: 276). Failing to do so, in our view, means that organisations cannot truly call themselves trauma-informed. Negotiating post-prison motherhood and attempting to re-establish a maternal role, while trying to repair a reduced maternal identity, presents significant challenges for mothers in their resettlement and in their desistance journey, no matter how resilient they were (Garcia-Hallett, 2019; Baldwin, 2022a). Successful reintegration and survival for post-prison mothers is assisted by informed support (Masson, 2019; Baldwin, 2022a; O'Malley et al, 2022), but it is not always available. If support is available, it often doesn't take into account motherhood, and the mothers have to rely on their own inner resources instead. As Dee, who had left her baby and other children 'outside' during her sentence, states:

> 'Yeah, it was a challenge to stay clean and straight, it was stressful coming back to being a full-time mum after prison and still having all the same shit to deal with as before but now worse ... and fighting to get my other kids back, yeah I could have done with some help with that. It was hard to cope, some days I didn't feel strong enough or you know, like I could do it, but I just had to ... because where was the help?' (Dee)

Conclusion

Reintegration into society and into the family after prison is always challenging (Codd, 2008; Masson, 2019; Booth, 2020; Baldwin, 2022a), but as this chapter shows, there are specific and unique challenges for post-release pregnant and/or new mothers. Moreover, some of those challenges intersect with desistance/re-entry to prison. We, like others (Mulligan, 2019; Baldwin et al, 2020; Martin and Powell, 2021), believe that even with the after-effects described here, it is still better for babies and toddlers to remain with their mothers wherever possible. However, it is important to reflect on why prison or separation are considered as first choices, when community-based solutions and/or mother and child residential units in the community exist or can be developed and are proven to be effective and appropriate. Maternal trauma and the maternal role must be factored into all post-prison support if mothers are to avoid repeated patterns. Baldwin has developed tools and training for probation officers who work with mothers to assist in this process and Birth Companions have also produced research, tools and guidance to support pregnant and new mothers who are criminal justice involved (prison and community).[6]

This chapter has described the painful reality of pregnancy and new motherhood in prison, revealing the significant turmoil, fears and everlasting impact beyond the prison walls. The costs of having been a prisoner lingers for many women (and their babies), with often devastating consequences. Illustrated painfully by Beth's suicide, and Michelle Barnes' suicide five days following the birth of her third child. We have also learnt how the trauma of birthing in prison cells not only hurts and traumatises the labouring woman but has significant emotional challenges for other women who may be sharing a cell or living on the same wing or houseblock (not to mention staff attending such events). This was particularly pertinent for Louise, whose baby Brooke-Leigh was tragically stillborn, and the friend who supported her in labour. We have also heard stories of strength and resilience through the complexities of being pregnant or a new mother in prison, with descriptions of hope and mental toughness. Despite the pain and hurdles of maternal imprisonment, the fact is that most women survive it. Women somehow find a resilience they often didn't know they had, to survive a system many of them shouldn't be in.

Let us for a minute 'pause for thought' and think how we could cope and keep going in similar circumstances, at the same time knowing we are asking that of others.

Pause for thought

- How has this chapter made you feel?
- Has this chapter made you feel differently about prison as a response to criminalised pregnant and new mothers?
- What can you do in your professional/personal life to make a difference?
- What do you think should be done?

The following chapter, Chapter Six, written by two mothers who are part of the Birth Companions Lived Experience Team, and who have lived experience of prison MBUs, will continue to reflect the reality of prison as a pregnant or new mother. Contextual discussion will be provided by Kirsty Kitchen, a member of the leadership team at Birth Companions.

SIX

Personal experiences of pregnancy and motherhood in prison and the value of the voluntary sector in challenging the system

Samantha Harkness, Michelle Wright and Kirsty Kitchen

'Please let my baby be OK.'

Michelle, 2022

Introduction

This chapter offers a view of the needs and experiences of pregnant women and mothers of infants in prison from two women who have lived it, and the charity that supported them during that time and beyond, namely Birth Companions. It considers the value of specialist, voluntary sector provision in prison, the need for scrutiny and for holding the state to account for its provision of care to women and babies in incarceration. It argues the case for a different approach to the sentencing of pregnant women and mothers. Ultimately, like the authors, we believe that, while improvements in the care of women who are pregnant or have recently given birth must be made, the prison environment will never be a safe and appropriate environment for those women and their babies, and that reform of the practices around remand, sentencing and licence recall is essential in order to bring an end to imprisonment for these women in all but the most exceptional of circumstances.

This chapter is co-authored by Samantha, Michelle and Kirsty; three members of the charity Birth Companions, which has specialised in supporting and advocating for pregnant women and new mothers in contact with the CJS for more than 25 years. Samantha and Michelle are members of the Birth Companions Lived Experience Team; a group of over 40 women who are committed to using their experiences of the criminal justice, social services and maternity systems to drive improvements in the care of other pregnant women and mothers. Kirsty is head of policy and communications at the charity, working closely with the Lived Experience Team to influence policy and practice across these systems.

The Birth Companions Lived Experience Team

The Lived Experience Team is a group of volunteers, many of whom have received Birth Companions' support themselves while in prison or in the community. Members of the team are recompensed for the work they do at the NHS Patient and Public Voice payment rates, in recognition of the expertise they bring to the projects they are involved in, including policy consultations, research, training and resource development. Where payments may have implications for a woman's welfare benefits, staff provide support on obtaining appropriate advice.

Together we have provided an overview of the way our organisation works and its impact, alongside creative writing and personal recollections of the prison environment. Throughout the chapter, 'Pauses for Thought' prompt students and professionals to reflect and consider as a means of developing their own views and practices in this area.

We hope that by reading this chapter you will develop a sense of the ways that policy, guidance and systems cultures impact on women's lives, the very real consequences of actions or failures to act, and the ways in which we can enact positive change in often intransigent settings to break cycles of trauma and disadvantage.

About Birth Companions

Birth Companions is a women's charity dedicated to tackling inequalities and disadvantage during pregnancy, birth and early motherhood. We were founded in 1996 to support pregnant women and new mothers in Holloway Prison. Since then we have become experts in meeting the needs of women living in the most challenging situations in prison and in the community.

The women we support face many difficulties which can often make the birth of their baby a time of anxiety, stress and hardship. These can include being in contact with the CJS, involvement with social services, immigration issues, homelessness, poverty, mental ill-health and a history of domestic violence or sexual abuse. Time and again our work has shown that with the right support cycles of disadvantage can be broken, and the futures of mothers and their babies improved. We are led by and for women, and many of those we support go on to join our Lived Experience Team so that together we can achieve real change in the way women and their babies are cared for across the UK and beyond.

The diary excerpts in this chapter were written by Michelle as she navigated her experience of the CJS. The entries illustrate the pain and anxiety incarcerated mothers feel as they are catapulted into the prison system. Michelle says of these excerpts that she feels they "speak for many more women than myself".

Dear Diary,

I'm terrified.

I arrived into prison today with no idea what to expect or that I would even be here. I was told a custodial sentence wouldn't be on the cards.

It's cold and the prison guards are colder. I was searched. Drug tested. Had to pee in a pot for a pregnancy test. They asked did I know, I said yes. They told me nothing. Gave me nothing.

Sent to a waiting room, my blood was pumping cold through my veins. Waiting to be called for whatever came next. I had no idea what that was. The other women in the room had been here before. Chatting like it was a coffee morning. They didn't really pay any attention to me; besides telling me I'll be OK.

Eventually my name was called, and I was asked my dress size, given ill-fitted grubby clothes from the prison storeroom and handed a clear plastic bag to see me through the first two weeks. This included a toothbrush, Pringles and a comb among other things.

We were escorted to the wings as a group and I was shown to a steel door upstairs on the induction wing, as it would be called. The stale stench of cigarettes made me heave and she soon shut the door behind me, leaving me with tobacco stained pillows and duvets to make up.

I'm so scared; I called my mum and begged her to help me. What if the stress causes me to miscarry? What if I get punched in the stomach?

Please let my baby be OK.

Michelle

Our approach to building engagement

As a voluntary sector organisation we are uniquely placed to engage with women – many of whom have experienced acute disadvantage, trauma and abuse in their lives – who may be reluctant to work with statutory service providers. That reluctance can be rooted in many things, including mistrust of professionals in statutory roles; a fear of repercussions in terms of social services involvement and the loss of children to care proceedings; and a sense of resignation and distance developed from previous experiences of being 'let down', judged or stigmatised (Baldwin, 2021a, 2021b, 2022b). As a charity focused on working with women on the basis of their pregnancy and their mothering identity, putting mothers' needs above all else, we are able to overcome many of the barriers faced by other services. Building these bridges can mean better engagement across the board, which can have an impact on positive outcomes for mothers and their babies.

We do this through a commitment to three core values; we are woman-centred, trauma-informed and non-judgmental.

Pause for thought

Try to imagine for a second what it must feel like to enter prison pregnant.

- What would be worrying you most?
- Who would you look to for support?
- Why might women be reluctant to engage with support?
- How would you as a practitioner build trust with women in prison and what skills would help you do this?

Our services

Within our service models we build packages of support unique to each individual, spanning one or several of the following:

- One-to-one practical and emotional support for women during pregnancy and throughout early motherhood.
- Advocacy services, including helping women navigate contact with children's social services.
- Birth support for women who might otherwise give birth on their own.
- Practical essential items.
- Trauma-informed antenatal courses designed specifically to meet the needs of women in prison, and those experiencing disadvantage in the community.
- Mother and baby groups where women can make friends, take part in activities and access support from staff, volunteers and peer supporters.
- Support for women experiencing bereavement and loss through miscarriage, stillbirth and separation from their children.
- Support for women accessing abortions.
- Peer support programmes.

Understanding and communicating the impact of prison in pregnancy/early motherhood

Our proximity to women and the issues they face in prison on a daily basis – from problems getting maternity bras and fresh fruit to missed antenatal appointments due to a lack of prison escorts, or births in cells – means we are also uniquely placed to challenge the system and drive change through bringing matters to the attention of policy makers and into the public domain. Prisons, by their very nature, limit the degree to which people can see and challenge what's happening, or to report poor practice and identify systemic trends and deficiencies. Thankfully, Birth Companions has been and continues to be able to draw on our current case work with women to highlight issues at local, regional and national levels that may otherwise have gone unrecognised. We think of this as 'letting the light in'.

For more than 25 years we have worked tirelessly to drive improvements in the care of pregnant women and mothers of infants in the CJS, learning much about the drivers of and barriers to change along the way. We've met with prisons ministers; worked closely with HMPPS Women's Team, NHS Health & Justice, the PPO, the justice inspectorates, the Magistrates Association, as well as individual prisons, in order to shape policies, standards and guidance based on what we know is working, and failing, on the ground. Often attention in the media helps ensure these conversations happen or are given the focus they require.[1]

As a result of this work, and catalysed by the tragic deaths of three babies, one stillborn in an ambulance en route to hospital (2017), and two further stillbirths in English prisons in the space of just nine months (PPO, 2021, 2022), there is now an unprecedented level of attention. This attention and the *Review of Operational Policy on Pregnancy, Mother and Baby Units and Maternal Separation*[2] (2020) has resulted in improved standards, and specific policy and guidance on the care of women experiencing pregnancy, pregnancy outcomes (including miscarriage, stillbirth, abortion and ectopic pregnancy), birth, maternal separation and time on MBUs. These are significant steps forward, but unless this attention can translate into meaningful and consistent changes at a practical and national level in a system we know is already overstretched and will continue to be primarily punitive and security-driven, the results may still fall far short of the rhetoric.

All these changes, and in particular the publication of the prison service's first policy framework on pregnant women and mothers of children up to the age of two (Ministry of Justice and HMPPS, 2021), will need to be able to address the dominant themes we and many others have drawn attention to in the prison estate. These include the impact of shame and guilt (Baldwin, 2015, 2017), the prevalence of trauma and the extent to which this can be triggered by pregnancy, birth and in the postnatal period (Abbott, 2018). Positive change is also required in meeting women's needs around mental health (Dolan, 2018), the acute fear of social services involvement (Baldwin et al,

2022a, 2022b), the consequences of maternal separation (Powell et al, 2017; MBRRACE-UK, 2021; Abbott et al, 2023a) and the significant risks related to pregnancy complications, birth and postnatal care in the prison environment (Abbott, 2018). Echoing previous research (Baldwin and Epstein, 2017; Abbott, 2018; Davies et al, 2021; Baldwin, 2022a), recent research by Epstein et al (2022) has returned into sharp focus the sheer levels of health and social care need experienced by pregnant women in prison. The report further highlights that pregnant women, entering the prison system through remand, sentence or recall, are disadvantaged and let down in terms of their maternal care needs. The report offered a reminder that many of the mothers' needs are exacerbated rather than addressed in the prison system, with major risks presented to mother and baby (Epstein et al, 2022). As has been previously stated, most women are imprisoned as a result of nonviolent offences and only a short period of incarceration, so why, we and so many ask, are these women entering the system in the first place (Baldwin and Epstein, 2017; Birth Companions, 2021)?

Our staff, volunteers and Lived Experience Team members work closely together, alongside campaigners, practitioners and academics, to explore this question with those in positions of power, seeking to challenge and positively disrupt the current system and to question judicial responses to pregnant women and new mothers. We hope that the momentum we are able to build together will continue to bring public attention to the current situation, the impact on mothers and their children, and the alternatives, which we will explore further at the end of the chapter.

Samantha's experience

It's really coincidental that I am writing this around my son's birthday. This month and the time surrounding his birthday is always an emotional time for me. I always go back to where he was born and how many years ago that was. The guilt hits me ten times harder in the run up to his birthday and I always feel like I must make his birthdays super magical.

This is because I was six months pregnant with my son when I was remanded to custody for my first ever offence; a non-violent one, I would add. I mention it was my first offence and non-violent because so many people assume everyone in prison is there because they pose a danger to others, so it's the only option. It's just not true. Many pregnant women and mothers have been in the exact same position as me and been sent to prison with no thought or chance of community sentencing nor rehabilitation and many women suffer the lifelong effects of these traumatic situations. I am one of them.

I was sent to prison on remand, less than 24 hours from being arrested I found myself sitting in a van being taken to prison. I was angry that there was no consideration taken for the fact I was clearly pregnant, and I was upset that I was going to be locked up in a prison and concerned for mine and my son's safety. I had no idea what I was facing but it was a very scary time and I felt very vulnerable. Throughout my time in prison it was the other prisoners who helped me. I had no support, no information, and had to rely on those other women not the staff to help me. It was them who told me about procedures that should be happening (but weren't). They were the ones who would give me their fruit ration for the day, so I could get some nutrients for my unborn child, because the prison wouldn't give me extras. Mentally I blocked out what was going on around me and just kept my head down and hoped I would be going home with my son. But I didn't.

My labour started In the early hours of the morning, and I pressed the call bell in my cell at 5am and told the night officer that I thought I had started labour. I was told someone would be with me shortly, but it was two hours later, and a couple more calls on the bell before I heard the keys unlock the door. It was the same time they unlocked the rest of the landing. I assumed it would be medical help, but it was the daytime officer that had taken over and didn't know I was in labour. By this time I was in a lot of pain. The prison nurse was called, and she had to confirm I was in labour in order for them to call an ambulance, arrange two officers to escort me and get me out the prison. She did this by taking my blood pressure; that's it. She wasn't trained to care for a pregnant woman. It was five hours from when I first told them I was in labour to when an ambulance was called, and I was finally taken to hospital. I was cuffed and walked through the hospital entrance like I was paraded as a freak show for all to see while clearly heavily pregnant.

When my son was born I was sent on to a mother and baby unit in another prison. Them places are a curse and a blessing. They aren't safe for children but gave me the opportunity not to be separated from my son. I was there for a week, and I broke down and couldn't do it. I couldn't keep him in there. I called my solicitor and asked for a bail application. I didn't apply for bail before this, because I was told the chances were slim and I didn't want to get my hopes up. I also thought it might affect my chances of getting a place on a mother and baby unit and I would lose my son forever. He was the only thing getting me through this. But when I did decide to apply, bail was granted, and I went home the following day. But mine and my son's journey through the criminal justice system was far from over.

We went home for three months while I awaited sentencing. It was like being in a dream all while having my imminent sentencing date looming closer and closer and not knowing if I would have to leave my baby and go back to prison.

The day of sentencing came, and I kissed my son goodbye and cried the whole way to court, not knowing when I would see him again. I had to do that three times as sentencing kept being adjourned. Each time it felt like someone ripped my heart from my chest.

I wrote a letter to the judge and pleaded with him to spare me a jail sentence to allow me to stay with my son. I asked if prison was the only option, and that he please take into consideration my son and the fact that mother and baby unit (MBU) rules stated you could only keep your child with you in the prison up to when they reach 18 months old. My pre-sentence report also stated I shouldn't get a custodial sentence. He sent me straight to prison. My first offence, first time I had even been arrested, and here I was going to serve a custodial sentence.

Once I was back inside I was able to apply for another place on the MBU but that process took five weeks to get into place and I had no certainty there would be a space for me or where in the country that could be. Meanwhile my mum was looking after my son and had to take leave from work. My parents would bring my son to visit but as they left he would cry, and I would be a mess, so I stopped the visits because they were unbearable for both of us and my mental health was all over the place. Those were the darkest days of my life and had I not been able to get back on the unit and have my son with me then I might not be here to tell my story.

We finally went onto the MBU, and I was so happy to have my son back and be able to feed him, change his bum, bath him, cuddle him, put him to bed and just be able to stare at his face. He was with his mummy, where he should be, but then I would turn my head and look at the metal bars that covered the windows and wonder if I made the right decision and feel an enormous amount of guilt that my son was serving this sentence with me. That doesn't go away when you're released, it doesn't go away as the years pass, it's there forever. You just learn to deal with it better. I couldn't put into words the amount of tears I have cried during and after my experience of the criminal justice system and becoming a mother.

While in the MBU I felt like a lot of decisions were taken from me as a mother. We saw a health visitor once a week and she made the decision if we was allowed to start weaning our children and if she said no, it was a no. Most of the women on the unit had other children so they knew from experience what their children needed but we was all treated like we was incapable of making decisions for our children. If we thought our child should see a doctor, we had to go through a member of the nursery staff and if they agreed then they had to make the call and speak to the doctor and make arrangements for the child to visit the doctor outside (not the prison doctor) and often a member of the nursery staff would have to take the child instead of the mother because the prison was so short staffed they couldn't free up two officers to escort them. Such a bittersweet situation – you wanted them to get medical attention when they needed it but having them taken out by someone else was so hard. I wish nobody would have to go through that. Waiting for a phone call from a stranger about the health of your child, could you imagine?

Approaching the end of my sentence I realised that I had been eligible for ROTL. No one had told me. ROTL would of allowed me to take my son outside of the prison walls and return with him. Even if it was to the local park, it was something I had craved for 11 long months. These opportunities had been taken away from me and my son. I was so angry and upset that my son had missed the chance to experience the world outside the prison because nobody had bothered to sort the paperwork out. When I had been asking questions about it I was sent round in circles and never got a straight answer. It became clear there had been a mistake when my electronic home detention curfew (tag) application was put through a lot faster than normal, and we was finally allowed home with curfew restrictions. They could of locked me in the house all day as long as I got to take my boy out of that place.

My son had his first birthday in prison … how will I ever tell him that or explain that to him? How will I ever find the right words to apologise that my son had to pay for my mistakes? No trips to the park, no feeding the ducks, no walks to the shops. The simple things that I now make sure we never take for granted.

In focus: equivalence of care

A key question prompted by reflection on the acute needs associated with pregnancy, birth and motherhood in prison is the degree to which the principle of equivalence of care is or will ever be possible in the estate. The government and NHS's commitment to equivalence of care is set out as

> the aim of ensuring that people detained in prisons in England are afforded provision of and access to appropriate services or treatment … and that this is considered to be at least consistent in range and quality (availability, accessibility and acceptability) with that available to the wider community, in order to achieve equitable health outcomes and to reduce health inequalities between people in prison and in the wider community. (National Prison Healthcare Board, 2019)

As outlined in Chapter One, the PPO report into the death of Baby Brooke (Baby B) in HMP Styal (PPO, 2021) found that when her mother Louise began experiencing acute abdominal pain and vaginal bleeding in her prison cell (she was, unknowingly, pregnant after having her drink spiked) the senior prison officer who attended her called the healthcare department three times. Three times, the nurse on duty declined to visit Louise, and didn't check her records or prescribe pain relief. At 9.06pm Louise gave birth to Brooke in a prison toilet.

The baby was delivered breech, and unresponsive. The guards radioed for an ambulance, but the radio system went down, so there was a delay in calling an ambulance, and prioritising the response. No attempt at resuscitation was made.

In the subsequent inquiry report, a consultant obstetrician said that if Louise had been taken to hospital earlier in the day they would have identified the baby was in the breech position and provided expert help with the delivery. She also stated that assuming Brooke was alive during the delivery (which Louise is convinced she was), the outcome 'would have been very different'.

Was Louise and Brooke's care equivalent in terms of access to and provision of appropriate services and treatment? Whether or not the pregnancy was known about, the response to Louise's presentation on the day/night of birth was, by these standards, worse than what she would have experienced in the community. Only because she was in prison did Louise have to rely on a prison officer relaying her medical need to a healthcare professional, rather than being able to speak directly to the nurse or phone an ambulance herself or taking herself to hospital. The barriers arising from poor practice and a system that struggles to support prisoners' basic health (Health and Social Care Committee, 2018; Davies et al, 2021), that privileges security over safety, meant prompt and appropriate care, including basic pain relief, was denied to her on multiple occasions.

Were Louise and Brooke's outcomes equitable? This was at least the third baby to die in custody in England since 2017 (Baldwin, 2021b). One in ten women who give birth during their time in prison deliver their baby in their cell or on the way to the hospital (Davies et al, 2021). Poor care, and the risks created by the prison system, exacerbate rather than improve the already poor outcomes associated with existing health inequalities: women in prison are twice as likely to give birth to a premature baby that needs special care and five times more likely to have a stillbirth (*Observer*, 2021).

Michelle's diary entry painfully and powerfully reveals the indignity forced upon many women in prison, treated as so many describe 'like second class citizens' (Baldwin, 2021b: 302):

Dear Diary

I bled today.

The wings are open on a weekend. There's no gym or classes so we are all free to socialise and mingle. I don't fancy that today, so I've started a new book.

I needed a wee, so put my book down and closed the cell door. When I wiped there was blood and I panicked, my heart started racing and I thought 'please let everything be OK'.

I went straight down the stairs to the prison officer on duty that happened to be friendlier to me than the others.

He called the nurse, and I went to wait for her in my cell.

She wasn't quick, it's agonizing not knowing what's happening and that as a pregnant woman I'm not important enough for an emergency visit. My anxiety is setting in quickly and it's hard to breathe.

She arrived around 30 minutes later and asked me to lay on my cell bed with door open, with my legs apart so she could examine me.

I can't believe this is happening – this cannot be allowed?

I saw two male prison guards walking around the wings and the other inmates freely passing to each other's cells, past mine and all have a clear view – of me.

I refused and told her for privacy's sake she needs to close the door, which she didn't want to do. It took one of the male prison officers to stand outside my cell door while it was pushed closed to allow me to be examined in a humane and respectful manner as a pregnant woman scared she may be losing her baby.

The nurse left saying I was fine. I don't believe she even knew what she was doing or looking for. I've never felt so neglected and alone.

I want to be with my husband and be cared for properly. They don't care what happens here and my little baby is all I want looked after.

Michelle

Pause for thought

- What should have happened for Michelle?
- Do you think there is a view that 'prisoners' are less deserving of dignity?
- What do you think about this and how can you challenge this perception in your own role or practice?

Narrowing the gap between policy and practice

Out of concern about the continuing gap between policy and practice, Birth Companions has developed resources for both professionals and those who are pregnant or mothering in prison and those supporting them. Our Birth Charter Toolkit (Birth Companions, 2019) offers those working in the prison environment and those commissioning services within it a comprehensive guide to delivering against the principles set out in our influential Birth Charter, while our *Inside Guide to Pregnancy, Birth and Motherhood in Prison* (Birth Companions, 2020) is an engaging illustrated handbook for women and those around them, explaining what they should expect and who can help offer support every step of the way. Both are available on the Birth Companions website.[3]

Michelle's diary entry highlights the sense of shame described by many imprisoned pregnant women. It also reveals how rules designed around the needs and risk factors of the male estate have been replicated in the female estate without a gender-specific approach. While the guidance from HMPPS and the Ministry of Justice now clearly states that restraints are to be avoided for pregnant women wherever possible, there are still issues with officers refusing to remove handcuffs in hospital, and male officers remaining in the room during physical examinations, active labour and when women are starting to breastfeed their babies. All these issues have a profound impact on women's antenatal and postnatal experiences.

Dear Diary,

Today's the day I get to see my baby on a scan, and I can't stop crying. They slipped a piece of paper under my cell door about two weeks ago, details of the scan at the hospital, time etc. Of course I called my husband and he said he would be there. There was no mention on the letter that he couldn't and this is our baby.

It's not how I ever imagined, being handcuffed before one of the most special moments I'll ever get in my life. They handcuffed me in a taxi and walked me through the hospital to the waiting area. Every pair of eyes watching me like I had committed crimes far beyond human rationalization. I was sentenced to three months for a non-violent offence. Stop staring at me.

The female officer came in with me, I wasn't even granted a moment's grace to be with my baby and see her heartbeat. The feeling so overwhelming that she was OK, I cried and cried some more.

The next thing I knew the officers came barging in and told me my husband was here and I was not allowed my blood tests for baby and he was not allowed to be here, it was a security breach. What? Why was I not told this?

They made me feel like scum, shaking their heads and acting up completely out of line. I apologized and told them the letter hadn't said, so how was I to know? I said I didn't mean to cause an issue, this was our baby and that's what mattered.

I'm handcuffed and marched out of the hospital, people talking loudly 'that's her, look' and surrounded by prison officers, back up officers and security guards and put into a prison van to be escorted back.

They wouldn't let me have the bloods for my baby, how do I know everything is OK?

Please let me go home. I don't need to be here.

Michelle

Pause for thought

- How does the media portray criminalised mothers?
- What do you think your thoughts would have been if you had seen a pregnant mother handcuffed in an antenatal clinic?
- How do you think Michelle felt in this situation?
- What can/will you do in your role to challenge these negative perceptions?

Beyond prison walls

Of course, it's not just about what happens in prison. When women step through the gate on their day of release, or they leave court after a remand hearing, it can feel hugely daunting and overwhelming. The process of adjusting to life, and motherhood, outside prison walls can bring its own challenges and risks, no matter how much women have been looking forward to their release date (Eaton, 1993; Baldwin, 2022a). Mothers' descriptions of their attempts to navigate and rebuild their relationships with their children and families, and the impact of the guilt, shame and loss they have experienced, have demonstrated long-lasting trauma and 'collateral damage':

> [S]he smelt different, her hair was long, she knew words I hadn't taught her, her... just everything ... she even walked different. It's like ... when I got out I felt like I didn't know her, I felt like I didn't know my own child, like I didn't know what made her tick, I didn't know what food she liked or owt like that. And that's horrible, my own child and I don't even know this stuff about her. Like now I have caught up with it, her favourite colours, her favourite books, blah de blah ... but it made me feel depressed until I did ... and I still don't feel I get it right no more. (Sophie, Baldwin, 2022a: 200)

Pause for thought

- What opportunities or voice do women have to challenge poor professional practice in the prison estate?
- What support is or should be available for mothers post-release?
- What might prevent them from using those opportunities, where they exist?
- What can you do to support this?
- What are the potential consequences of not being supported post-release?

Samantha's experience

The day came for us to go home, and I always thought I would be jumping and cheering for joy but I was the opposite.

I had fears and worries and emotions I didn't realise I would. I hugged the women goodbye, waved to the nursery staff and gave one officer the middle finger as we walked out the gates. That certain officer made every single woman's life miserable in that unit. She wasn't a mother. She had no idea what we were feeling and how much all of us struggled. She constantly threatened us to have our places on the MBU taken away and the babies sent home and it could of been for the smallest thing like oversleeping after being up with our children all night.

The gates opened and I was stood there with one black hold-all and my son in his buggy. The sun was shining but it was a frosty morning. I heard 'take care of yourself and that handsome little fella' from the gatekeeper, I gave him a nod and a smile, and I stepped back into the real world. My dad was waiting for us and I burst into tears. He was so confused!

When you're released from prison everyone expects you to be happy but it's very scary. You're stripped of everything when you're in that system and it's almost like you have to find yourself again and learn how to be you. Even people being able to just call you up, it's overwhelming. I was used to contacting people on my terms, when I could talk, but then I was thrown into a situation where the phone would be ringing, the door would be knocking, I would be trying to make a bottle, the baby would be crying etc. This sent me into a depression. It was all too much at once and nobody understood why I wasn't happy to be home. I hated prison but at that time I wished I had been back in there. I kept all these feelings to myself and pushed people away because they expect you to be jumping for joy to be home but the whole experience was so traumatic that I am still dealing with it today and probably forever.

I have been home from prison a few years now. I still cry myself to sleep some nights because the guilt is just overwhelming. I worry my son will judge me and my mistakes. The day the judge remanded me to prison, and I had my son in custody … he handed me a life sentence.

Collateral damage

It's not only the emotional impact of time in prison, but the impact of the woman's removal from her society, her network and her possessions. Housing is a major issue, with 77 per cent of women released from the UK's largest female prison without safe and secure accommodation to go to (Independent Monitoring Boards, 2021). This has significant implications not only for women's rehabilitation but also for their opportunities to rebuild connections with their children and secure reunification if those children have been taken into care. Baldwin's research (2020a, 2022a), which explored the long-term impact of maternal imprisonment, found that post-release mothers struggled to deal with the consequences and trauma of separation from their children, or of being pregnant in prison, with women describing suffering from symptoms of PTSD for years, sometimes decades. We also argue that there are risks in focusing too much on pregnancy and motherhood *in* prison and not enough on the community criminal justice contexts like probation supervision, licence conditions after release, community sentences or women awaiting court outcomes.

Echoing Baldwin's (2022a) and Abbott's (2018) research, our research (Birth Companions, 2021) found a significant lack of recognition of, and responsiveness to, pregnancy and motherhood among probation services, and considerable impact on their antenatal and postnatal care needs resulting from their contact with the CJS. One woman described her pregnancy being ignored by her probation officer:

> Up until I had him I felt she [probation officer] cut the bump out, that is what I would say. If that was me and I was the probation [officer] I think I would take a little bit of compassion, maybe ask the woman how is she feeling about her pregnancy, how's things been going you know. (Birth Companions, 2021: 11)

Yet despite this mother's experience, the vast majority of the professionals surveyed in the Birth Companions research said they viewed pregnancy and early motherhood as particular opportunities to facilitate positive changes (Birth Companions, 2021), demonstrating the need for more focused, woman-centred approaches in community CJS agencies and specialist maternity care for women with CJS involvement. It is clear that we are currently losing these opportunities to support motherhood and to understand the ways in which motherhood can be interwoven with rehabilitation and desistance (Baldwin, 2022b).

Samantha's experience

I had to attend probation appointments weekly and the probation officer I had to begin with was very understanding and after a couple of months put me on to telephone contact as I always found it hard to find childcare to attend the appointments. This was short lived because I was given to another probation officer who insisted I had to attend the office weekly and continued to make me do that and travel to another town for a two-minute conversation. I was never a flight risk and they was all aware I had been released with my son, although looking back I think some people had an issue with the fact I had my son on MBU. Each to their own. They would never understand until they are faced with that decision.

I was sure my probation was due to end in the month of April and when I called the probation officer to ask this she told me she was unaware when my licence ended and I should carry on attending, so I did ... for another three weeks, until I found a copy of my licence and noticed I had been attending appointments for five weeks past the end date. It was the same day I was due to attend so I took great pleasure in calling her and telling her I won't be attending, and she said I would be arrested if I didn't. ... Never heard another word from her! Just another example of a failure in a flawed system!

Creative writing can be a useful outlet for mothers in and after prison, providing a healthy and lasting way of managing difficult and painful emotions. Michelle wrote this beautiful poem for her child.

Moments in time

Time is known to only exist in a single moment
To belong to us, before it doesn't anymore
We were handed a watch, you and I,
Handcuffed to the invisible, the impossible
Trapped inside an existence not meant for us

With the rising of the sun, tears of guilt arise from my heart
With the darkness of the moon, my soul grieves deeply
Time moves silently, what was, is and will be is all here,
I place my hand on my tummy to feel you,
To tell you how much I love you

Night by night, day by day
I close my eyes and picture your tiny fingers,
Wrapped around mine,
As we move forward the hands of time,

Hour by hour,
Minute by minute,
Second by second
Until we are free from their time and exist only in our own.

Michelle Wright

Conclusion

It is clear that, despite some good intentions and some recent progress in terms of the policy and guidance relating to pregnancy and early motherhood in prison, the barriers created by the system will continue to present significant risks to the health and wellbeing of women and their babies (O'Malley et al, 2021). It is vital that together we continue to shine a light on these barriers and their impacts, and that we scrutinise delivery against the new policies to ensure care is as good as it can be. Progress must be measured and reviewed while simultaneously driving fundamental reforms to the processes of remand, sentencing and recall, so that community-based alternatives are used in all but the most exceptional of cases. Prison will never be a safe place for pregnant women or the most appropriate space for babies; not when proven alternatives are available and effective. These alternatives, such as community sentence treatment requirements, suspended sentences and work with specialist services including women's centres have been shown to address the drivers of women's offending without placing mothers and babies at risk in a system fundamentally unsuitable for their care. Birth Companions will continue to lead and champion this conversation in professional and public spaces, with the goal of ensuring the best possible start for babies and the best future for mothers, no matter what their circumstances.

SEVEN

'Learning lessons': discussion, concluding thoughts and recommendations

'It's not rocket science, don't send pregnant women to prison for shoplifting.'

Beth, 2017

Introduction

All mothers take with them a legacy from their time in prison and/or a prison MBU. Sometimes that legacy is positive; for example, some mothers may have benefited from a safer and intentionally supportive space to begin life as a mother than they might otherwise have had (though most often not without some cost), but often there are negative and complex consequences too. This evidence-based volume has revealed and unpicked some of those realities.

We, the authors, have both undertaken multiple research projects that inform our writing here, but the bulk of the evidence for this book came from two main studies, *Motherhood Challenged* (Baldwin, 2021a) and *The Incarcerated Pregnancy* (Abbott, 2018). We acknowledge that since our research was undertaken there is more of an appetite and motivation for positive change (in part, stimulated and assisted by our research). This change, although coming on the back of the aforementioned tragedies, is welcome.

This chapter incorporates a reflective summary of the takeaway messages of the book while re-stating the current landscape and present commitment to change. Drawing on our own thoughts, research and the women's voices, we conclude with 21 recommendations, which, if implemented, we feel would go some way towards minimising harm and improving outcomes for pregnant and new mothers in and after prison.

Appetite for change

It is positive that the Ministry of Justice[1] has committed to improving conditions for mothers and their babies, and that they are heeding advice and guidance from experts like the authors, charitable organisations like Birth Companions and activists like the gender justice pressure group Level Up.[2] We echo the recommendations we have made previously, and those outlined in the recent reviews. The Trowler review and the *Review of Operational Policy on Pregnancy, Mother and Baby Units and Maternal Separation* are important and influential reports that shine a light on the current provisions made for mothers and babies, where the gaps in provision are and how best to improve responses. If fully implemented the recommendations and actions from both reports would make a significant difference to outcomes for mothers and babies. Furthermore, the Female Offender Strategy Delivery Plan[3] (FOSDP) 2022–2025, published in January 2023, opens with: 'When women with experiences of violence, poor mental health and addiction are left unsupported, society pays the price' (Ministry of Justice, 2023: 3). Society does indeed pay a price, but no price is higher than the mothers and their children pay. It is widely accepted that without improvements to social justice, tackling disadvantage and discrimination, there cannot and will not be improvements in criminal justice for women (Clarke and Chadwick, 2018: 51–71; Baldwin, 2022a). As the delivery plan rightly states and as we have shown in this book, 'many of the women who come into contact with the criminal justice system have experienced domestic abuse, mental health problems or have a history of alcohol and drug misuse. They often commit non-violent, low-level offences, for which many receive short custodial sentences' (FOSDP, 2023: 10).

Sentencing

It is known that women tend not to commit violent crime and, as the FOSDP states, women are 'over-represented in prosecutions for specific offences, particularly non-police prosecutions'. Often because it is women who are home or because they are single parents it is usually women who are prosecuted for TV licence evasion or truancy. Women are criminalised, as we have seen, for poverty, mental ill-health and trauma. The FOSDP states that in the year ending June 2022, women sentenced for theft, summary non-motoring offences and miscellaneous crimes against society also accounted for over half (58 per cent) of all women given custodial sentences of less than 12 months (2023: 10–11). Yet although it is known that imprisoning women often traps women in a cycle of further disadvantage, trauma, loss and reoffending (see Chapter Three), nonviolent women, including pregnant and new mothers, continue to be sent to prison. We know that for mothers and children separated at this key point in their lives, the implications can be serious and lifelong (Powell et al, 2017; O'Malley and Baldwin, 2019; Baldwin, 2020). For children separated from their mothers by imprisonment, the options are to be placed in kinship care or into state care (Baldwin, 2015). Some of these children will be placed for adoption and never reunited with their families (Choice for Change, 2015). There are no official records of children of female prisoners, or numbers of children in care and those who are permanently separated from their mothers (Galloway et al, 2014; Minson, 2021).

We know from Mary and the other mothers quoted herein, that the disruption to families, the loss of employment, accommodation, family ties and/or children can trigger a cycle of intergenerational criminal justice involvement. Despite decades of evidence that community sentences are less disruptive and more effective, women continue to be disproportionately affected and punished by maternal imprisonment. So what do we need to do? As Beth powerfully and sensibly stated before her tragic death: "It's not rocket science, don't send pregnant women to prison for shoplifting" (Beth). In their recent report (Epstein et al, 2022) 'Why are pregnant women still in prison?', a thought-provoking statement is made:

> Imprisonment for pregnant women is not necessary. It is a choice made by the legal system of each country. Eleven countries (with a total population of about 646 million) do not permit the imprisonment of pregnant women, or severely curtail the use of custody. They use options such as house arrest, electronic monitoring or the use of probation. Italy has enacted laws to protect pregnant women from entering prison, both on remand (pre-trial detention) and on sentence. (Epstein et al, 2022: 4)

This is an important point to consider and reflect on. Things do not have to be the way they are. There is no doubt that there has been much positive change in recent years, more than for many decades previously. There is a sense of a real commitment to positive change that had previously been absent; from the courts, from probation from the HMPPS women's team and policy directorate, and from prisons themselves. However, the fact remains that we still imprison too many women, via remand, recall and sentencing. The FOSDP (2023: 10) states that it will deliver[4] on four key priorities to reduce women's offending over the period of 2022–2025, further stating that action to deliver many of these commitments is already underway.

1. Fewer women entering the justice system and reoffending. In some cases, a women's offending could have been prevented through earlier intervention, including through diversion from the CJS and into support.
2. Fewer women serving short custodial sentences with a greater proportion managed successfully in the community.
3. Better outcomes for women in custody.
4. Better outcomes for women on release.

Further detail of how the government intends to deliver on the plan is within the FOSDP. The government stated in the recent FOSDP (2023: 10) that '[m]ore than four years on from the publication of the Female Offender Strategy, this Government remains committed to its three aims – earlier intervention and improved community sentences, reducing the number of women going to prison, and making custody more effective'. However, if the government is truly committed to reducing the number of women being sent to prison, we have to question the decision to build 500 more new prison spaces for women. The rhetoric is that the new facilities will have 'improved' conditions for mothers and their children and will permit overnight stays, improved contact and so on. There are several responses to this, but it has to be said that to 'improve' conditions for mothers and children, additional cell spaces do not need to be created. 'Improvements' can be made without increased capacity. Second, if fewer mothers were imprisoned there would be less need for improved facilities that bring children into prisons – the focus should arguably be on keeping mothers out of prison, not bringing their children into prison. Third, there ought to have been an at least equitable financial commitment to developing community-based resources and women's centres in the community.

Research has shown that gendered responses like women's centres are successful in terms of supporting women and interrupting offending cycles (Carlen and Worrall, 2004; Harding, 2020; Morley and Rushton, 2023). There needs to be a focus on the courts and sentencing practices to ensure that women who do enter custody truly are women for whom there would be no suitable, safe or appropriate alternative. We strongly argue that the 'threshold for custody'[5] principles be revised, and as Baldwin (Baldwin, 2022a) and Baldwin and Epstein (2017) have previously advocated for, that gendered sentencing guidelines should be developed and applied. This would reduce the number of women, to include pregnant and new mothers, in custody, which has to be a shared commitment and goal if we are to see some of the harms mentioned in this book reduced and removed.

Following calls for change in a vociferous campaign fronted by Level Up and backed by academics, practitioners and policy makers (including the Royal College of Midwives), we are delighted that the Sentencing Council have agreed to consult on pregnancy as a new mitigating factor, with a view to (potentially), amending the sentencing guidelines. This consultation will take place in 2023/2024.

Some examples of changes in prison

The Ministry of Justice *Review of Operational Policy on Pregnancy, Mother and Baby Units and Maternal Separation* made important recommendations for positive change (discussed in more detail later), and as a result, pregnancy and motherhood are featured more heavily in the training of prison officers.[6] Thus, in theory, all officers throughout the female estate should now be more considered, prepared and thoughtful in their approach to working with pregnant and new mothers in prison. We, the authors, each provide an additional annual training/awareness session to officers via the 'Unlocked Graduates' scheme, and Baldwin delivers additional training to Sodexo staff. We feel these additional sessions should be taught to all officers, but we welcome the advances to date, nonetheless. All women's prisons are now required to have a PMBLO. There are in some prisons midwives who have become experienced working with women in prisons, but that is often through historic experience, rather than having specific training in prison systems. However, the delivery of prison midwifery remains variable and inconsistent.

HMP Low Newton

One answer to the provision of more consistent care across the whole estate lies in the *Health Service Journal* award-winning HMP Low Newton Pathway.[7] This provision of maternity care sees a dedicated specialist prison midwife leading a multidisciplinary team and overseeing the care for all pregnant women and mothers who have birthed within the previous two years (whether or not the baby remains with them). This pathway followed the death of Michelle Barnes in 2015 (see Chapter One), a woman separated from her baby who died by suicide five days after giving birth. The new pathway demonstrates clear accountability in care provision for pregnant women in prison. The project consisted of a prison midwife with a dedicated caseload and protected time who coordinates all the maternity care. We advocate that this collaborative model, with protected time, should be consistently delivered in every prison. Evaluation suggests that maternal and infant health outcomes have improved since the changes; that there has been a reduced need to transfer women out of the prison for routine care; and that women feel the approach offers greater consistency of care.

HMP Peterborough

In most prisons in the female estate pregnant prisoners are housed in 'normal location' (on the general wings). If they have secured a space on the MBU pre-birth pregnant women may be moved onto the MBU for the last weeks of their pregnancies. Following an 18-month consultation with one of the authors (Baldwin) and the undertaking of the 'Motherhood Project',[8] Baldwin made the recommendation that 'wherever possible' pregnant mothers should be located on a single wing. HMP Peterborough (Sodexo not HMPPS), has for the last year trialled locating pregnant women in one wing led by a particularly experienced, committed, motivated and compassionate officer (women 'have the choice but are encouraged' to go to the pregnancy wing). Initial feedback on the trial is that it has worked well, and it is described by Bev Stevens (Women's Policy Lead, Sodexo) as 'safer':

> One of the simple things we have changed as a result of thinking more deeply about motherhood during this project, is thinking about where and how we look after pregnant women, we now think it make sense to look after pregnant women on one wing. We won't insist on it, but we will now always encourage pregnant mothers to go on (D) wing. It's better for the mothers, it's better for the staff and most importantly we think it's safer. (Stevens to Baldwin, 2022c: 30)

Significantly for the mothers, this also means they can be a source of support to each other. Ms Stevens has described how the mothers have benefited from having 'normal' conversations with other pregnant mothers, especially mothers pregnant with their first child, and have benefited from the comfort, support and reassurance of each other. The mothers Baldwin has spoken to on the wing said they preferred it, that it 'normalised' their pregnancy because they had access to other pregnant mothers and that made it a 'less lonely' experience, something which is important and especially during a significant and emotional part of a woman's life. HMP Peterborough has no plans to end the trial and is looking to expand the plan to HMP Bronzefield, whilst also continuing to think of ways of positively supporting pregnant prisoners and maintaining their commitment to support mothers in prison.

Integrating pregnant women in a designated wing offers numerous benefits, including streamlined medical appointments, improved access to healthcare and consistent supply of specialised provisions. The presence of trained officers enhances safety and reduces staff stress levels. Interacting with other pregnant women provides normalisation and social support. This initiative addresses concerns raised in both of our previous research regarding provision issues. Thus, centralising pregnant women in one designated space offers various advantages, including better preparation, efficient resource distribution, faster access to healthcare services and mutual support among the mothers. HMP Peterborough plans to continue and expand the trial, with potential implementation in other prisons, as the HMPPS Women's Lead considers endorsing it for the entire prison estate. While the goal is reducing the number of pregnant women in prison, the pregnancy wing aims to mitigate issues and support the women during their time in custody.

We believe that the model of a 'pregnancy wing' could be developed and adapted for other prisons, with officers on the wing having additional and specific training to enable them to work with pregnant women in prison more confidently. We acknowledge it is unlikely that all prisons will be able to dedicate a whole wing space to only pregnant women because of the overall relatively low number of pregnant women in prison at one time. Thus, although possible to locate all pregnant women in one space, in some prisons there may be a need to place other women prisoners on the wing also. We would ask that careful consideration be given to who this group of women are. Baldwin (2022a) found in her research that older women in prison, who are often grandmothers, benefit from forming friendships and being able to 'mother' younger fellow prisoners. Ergo, it could be that older women prisoners deemed to be low risk and without convictions of violence, would be a good pool to draw from. The pregnant prisoners, as they did in Baldwin's research, could then potentially benefit from the support and guidance of older women – which in the absence of their own mothers (noted by Abbott [2018] as significant) could prove beneficial to wellbeing for both parties.

Safer but still not better

We are aware that there have been at least two 'safe' prison births in the last 12 months – and it is to the credit of the mothers and prison staff that the births went as smoothly as a prison birth can. Most important, that the mothers and babies concerned are safe and well. However, these births should never have happened. Although the births had safe outcomes, they will not have been without anxiety and trauma for the mothers (or the staff). There will be a legacy for all. The mothers concerned, as this book has shown, are likely to forever be dreading answering that question all children seem to ask eventually, 'Mummy, where was I born?'.

As has been illustrated by the mothers in this book and by Ms A and Louise's experiences, giving birth as a mother who is currently imprisoned has specific challenges. Even with the improvements made to perinatal pathways and improved care for pregnant mothers following the recent review, some of those challenges are not reduced and/or cannot be mitigated within the current 'rules'. For example, time taken to get in and out of prison, restraints during transport, officer presence, restrictions on when partners are allowed to be with a labouring mother, restrictions on number of birth partners and who they are. Mothers have described how these things, and the added discomfort of "feeling very much more like a prisoner than a new mum" (Paige), 'taint' or 'ruin' their birth experience, and not only for them but for their partners and families too. This all has an impact on the new mothers and, arguably, such stress at an already emotional time can increase the risk of birth trauma and postnatal depression. One of the mothers in

Baldwin's 'Motherhood Project' described how her birth had been distressing and uncomfortable because of a combination of challenges linked to her prisoner status. She described her birth as a 'circus'.

> Two officers were in the actual room whilst I gave birth – not outside the room even but in the room – same for breast feeding, eyes on you all the time. It was stressful and awful. My partner wasn't allowed in until I was pushing, he had been in the hospital car park waiting to be let in for 12 hours, but they literally kept saying no not until she's pushing. (Baldwin, 2022c: 33)

During the 'Motherhood Project' at HMP Peterborough, mothers' concerns and experiences were taken back and raised with senior management and Women's Policy Lead, Ms Stephens, who then made several immediate positive changes as a result of the feedback given from Baldwin's meetings on the MBU and the motherhood focus groups. Ms Stevens and HMP Peterborough have made the decision that 'wherever possible' (bearing in mind risk factors/timing/planning), mothers will give birth on ROTL: 'As a result of our [meaning LB and BS] meetings and discussions, our first woman gave birth on ROTL – we hope that now will be our standard, but we hadn't done that before and that now means women will have as normal a birth as possible' (Baldwin, 2022c: 33). This has and will continue to make a huge difference to mothers. Given that mothers will effectively be on leave from the prison during their births and immediately afterwards, they can now enjoy a birth as close to what they would have had if they were not in prison. Meaning the all-important bonding period between mother and child is less stressful, less observed and much more natural. We hope and recommend that this policy will be extended to the rest of the female estate enabling all imprisoned women to give birth in the community.

HMP Bronzefield

In the wake of the death of Aisha Cleary (Baby A), Sodexo/ Bronzefield conducted two internal investigations, one looking at operational issues and one at healthcare issues. As a result of issues identified by the PPO investigation and the two Sodexo investigations, Bronzefield has made a number of changes to policy and practice (see PPO report for a full list).[9] These changes (among others) included hourly checks for all pregnant women in their third trimester, revised and updated perinatal pathway guidance, and a fortnightly review board, attended by midwives, healthcare and operational staff, which provides a coordinated oversight of pregnant prisoners. The 'Motherhood Project' (led by Baldwin) recommendations that have been implemented at HMP Peterborough (also ran by Sodexo), are also likely to be rolled out into Bronzefield. Since the publication of the PPO report, Dr Christy Pitfield, Principal Clinical Psychologist and Clinical Lead for Perinatal Mental Health, Health & Justice Directorate Central and Northwest London NHS Foundation Trust, who also works out of Bronzefield, has told us of other ongoing work regarding perinatal mental health at Bronzefield. She told us that pregnant women in prison who access the perinatal mental health services (now commissioned for two years) typically have complex attachment histories, including early developmental and later adult trauma, and therefore often present with severe and enduring mental health needs. It is also not uncommon for patients who use the service to have experienced a history of complex perinatal or child losses of multiple types, alongside domestic violence and substance misuse difficulties, predisposing them to further vulnerability within the perinatal period. Thus, states Dr Pitfield, 'the ethos is that the point in which we meet such women is a window of opportunity to treat perinatal mental health and the impact of trauma, also and that we are making an important contribution to disrupting the intergenerational transmission of trauma' (email correspondence). Dr Pitfield then goes on to say that the service offers multidisciplinary perinatal mental health assessment and treatment to women during pregnancy; those who give birth while in custody; and those who reside with their infants on the MBU at HMP Bronzefield. A range of therapeutic interventions are then offered and available. Moreover, there is additional emphasis on providing training, supervision and consultation to the environment to support the wellbeing of women in prison. Dr Pitfield is also looking to develop reflective practice for officers working with pregnant women and mothers on the MBU, a clinical pathway for women who are separated from their baby during the perinatal period (much needed), and how best to support transgender individuals through their pregnancy journey.

The importance of community/hospital midwives understanding the prison context

Although we hate the phrase (because it often comes after an avoidable harm and is often ineffective and ignored), 'lessons must be learned' in the community too. Hospital obstetric teams and midwives based in the community must appreciate that sending a women 'home' is very different from sending women back to prison. It may well be that, especially for first-time mums, women may come to the labour ward with plenty of time to spare and ample time to return home and back safely farther down the line if they have been deemed to have arrived 'too soon'. However, for pregnant prisoners there are protocols, processes and permissions both getting back into the prison, but also out again, to go through. All of which take 'time', sometimes several hours, thus sending a pregnant prisoner back to prison in labour, even early labour, significantly increases the chances of her having a prison-based birth. If such an event were to occur (and is in fact exactly what happened in one of the fortunately safe births described earlier), then that would likely result in a birth not attended by a qualified midwife or obstetrician. Which can, as illustrated by the tragic events of Ms

A and Ms B's births, can have terrible and fatal consequences. If current practices are to remain unchanged, in our opinion it is a matter of time before we have another tragic death of a newborn baby, a mother or both.

The social work role

When the separation of social work and probation officer training occurred in the 1990s, social work lost its criminal justice influence and conversely probation work became less welfare orientated and more focused on risk, monitoring and punishment. As a result, both probation and social work lost something of itself in terms of knowledge and understanding of the context of the other. Social work and probation areas of work became more siloed. In recognition of the consequences of this loss, Baldwin (2015, 2021a, 2022c) (who under the old qualification scheme, that was the postgraduate Diploma in Social Work, is dually social work and probation officer trained and experienced); has long argued for the development of a new branch of criminal justice social work to be developed in England and Wales (it already exists in Scotland). Baldwin, among others, in her evidence to the Farmer Review, argued strongly for the role of social workers in prisons. This is particularly important since the probation service changed its focus from more relationship, welfare and rehabilitation-based work, to becoming more punitive and risk focused and orientated. Many prisons have long since lost these resident welfare-focused probation officers, leaving much of the 'welfare' work being left to overburdened officers, working in understaffed conditions. Thus, meaning many opportunities to work holistically with prisoners has been lost or reduced (some prisons retained probation officers, and a few had resident social workers, but not all). Acting on the evidence verbal and written of Baldwin and others (O'Malley and Devaney, 2016; Raikes, 2018 – see Farmer, 2019), Lord Farmer recommended a pilot of social workers in two women's prisons. Although only one year in at the time of writing, the pilot has gone well and made a significant difference to the experiences of some mothers in prison (Baldwin et al, 2022b; Rees et al, 2023). The Ministry of Justice announced in January 2021 that it had secured funding for the expansion of the scheme to three more female prisons. We suggest that an important part of this role could be assisting with MBU applications and assessments and providing a bridge between 'inside' and 'outside' social work, and thereby assist in creating a transferable and comprehensive support and care plan. We hope that if pregnant women continue to end up in prison (our preferred option will always be that they don't), then as more social workers become familiar with the often very positive surroundings and supportive environment of an MBU, they will be more accepting and willing to support mothers in their applications to remain with their babies. Meaning fewer babies will end up in the care system – which can only have more positive outcomes in the long and the short term, for mothers, their babies and society in general. Particularly as evidence has shown that mothers who spend time on an MBU and have the opportunity to bond and remain with their babies are far less likely to return to prison than those who did not or those who are in a normal location in the prison. We will never know for sure, but perhaps if social workers had been in prisons when Michelle was having her baby, she may have been supported to keep her baby, with very different outcomes.

Probation and multi-agency support

The relationship between motherhood and desistance is a complicated one (Bachman et al, 2016; Baldwin, 2021a, 2022a, 2022b). Research has produced mixed and confounding evidence about the relationship between motherhood and desistance (Bachman et al, 2016), however there would seem to be little doubt that motherhood places increased strain that add to the already difficult post-release desistance/re-entry journey for women (Eaton, 1993; Baldwin, 2022a; see also Brown and Bloom, 2009; Leverentz, 2014; Baldwin, 2022a). This book has demonstrated the dangers for women/mothers when they become trapped in cycles of trauma and maternal trauma. It has shown how missed and lost opportunities to support women in their motherhood can lead to repeated imprisonment and sometimes repeated loss of children. The importance of factoring in motherhood into probation supervision and/or multi-agency support cannot be overstated. Substance misuse agencies need to actively understand and factor in motherhood and maternal emotion, and how this can interact with substance use. Working together to understand and support mothers in a non-judgemental and collaborative way is vital to preventing more and more women becoming embedded in the CJS. Baldwin has produced training and tools for probation officers to use in their supervision with women. Baldwin's research provided evidence for the justification and effectiveness of such tools when working with mothers under supervision (Baldwin, 2022a, 2022b). Supporting community-based women's centres, and agencies like Birth Companions and PAUSE,[10] to work proactively and preventatively with women is vital to reducing the number of pregnant and new mothers in prison, and the numbers of babies and children in care.

Developing a maternal identity

Mothers in both our research (Abbott, 2018; Baldwin, 2021a, 2021b, 2022), described how being a pregnant mother in prison denied them the opportunity to rehearse motherhood or prepare for motherhood and begin to develop a 'maternal identity'. Thus, pregnant women in prison do not always go through the *process* of 'becoming a mother' in the way that free mothers do, via attending antenatal classes or buying baby clothes or preparing a nursery or bonding and making friendships with other pregnant mothers (Abbott, 2015: 20). This can have a profound effect not only on a mother's maternal emotions and identity, but also on the mother–child bond, which can have lifelong implications (Arendell, 2000; Abbott et al, 2020; Baldwin, 2021a: 168; O'Malley et al, 2022). We must do more to help mothers develop or hold on to that maternal identity even, if not especially, while in prison. We make a number of recommendations at the end of this chapter but also advocate for the changes highlighted here and implemented at HMP Peterborough to be rolled out more widely.

Ongoing commitments to positive change

As members of the Ministry of Justice National Advisory Forum for Pregnancy and MBUs, we are aware of a keen commitment to improve conditions and provisions for pregnant and new mothers in prison. The recently published FOSDP specifically mentions additional intent around pregnant mothers in prison and on an MBU. Importantly, the document states its commitment to mothers and motherhood more generally too. We are very keen to see this commitment come to fruition and will continue to contribute to developments through our research evidence and our roles on the advisory board. The Ministry of Justice (2018) has provided guidance for working with pregnant and new mothers in custody and in the community.[11] This document has since been updated and added to by the Women's Policy Framework (2021)[12] and the FOSDP, 2022–2025, published in January 2023.[13]

Birth Companions have contributed significantly to the landscape of positive change and development in perinatal care and criminal justice. The 'Birth Charter for Women in Prison' was published in 2016 'in response to long-held concerns about the risks faced by pregnant women, mothers and their babies in prison'. Birth Companions highlighted the then urgent need for improved standards of care for women and babies in custody and a 'complete lack of provision for them in policy and practice'. The 2016 Charter set out 15 principles of care relating to pregnancy, birth and the postnatal period in prisons.

Birth Companions 'hoped these principles would be taken up and used to form the basis of much-needed mandatory standards of care, set out in a Prison Service Instruction or equivalent'. Birth Companions recently published a summary of the positive impact of its 2016 Birth Charter.[14] The important and productive work of Birth Companions will continue. We are aware that Birth Companions will be contributing to work led by the Sentencing Council to review the sentencing guidelines as they relate to women, and to consider developing a specific mitigating factor on pregnancy.

Hibiscus[15] states that it works with women by 'empowering and championing the rights of foreign national and black, minority ethnic and refugee women and families at the intersection of the immigration and criminal justice systems'. Hibiscus works directly with marginalised migrant women at every point within the criminal justice and immigration system, supporting women at every opportunity on their difficult journey through the system, not specifically with but including pregnant and new mothers in the community, and in custody (prisons and detention centres).

Level Up is a feminist community campaigning for gender justice in the UK. Level Up has an active campaign for a change in the law to end the imprisonment of pregnant women, stating:

> The government can and must put an end to imprisoning pregnant women and new mothers by changing sentencing laws. Right now, there is no statutory duty for judges to take pregnancy or parenthood into consideration when sentencing. This has to change. The law needs to be strengthened so that judges legally have to consider the health of pregnant women and their babies and avoid sending them to prison at all costs.[16]

As well as being part of the National Advisory Forum, the authors also have a number of ongoing research and practice projects. Baldwin is engaged in the second phase of the 'Motherhood Project' with Sodexo, and a similar project in Ireland, as well as a qualitative study exploring the experiences of mothers on probation. Abbott founded the PMAG, which connects and support prison midwives across the female estate. The PMAG also feeds into the Pregnancy in Prison Partnership (International), again (co-)founded by Abbott. The Pregnancy in Prison Partnership (International) aims to improve the wellbeing of incarcerated pregnant women through international collaboration. Abbott also has recently launched her Economic and Social Research Council New Investigator funded 'Lost Mothers Study Project'. The project is exploring the effects of mandatory separation of babies from women with CJS involvement. Baldwin is on the Advisory Board of the project.

In our work with mothers we have heard mothers describe being arrested or being in court pregnant, sometimes visibly so, not knowing they were able to take a baby into prison – at least two of those women planned abortions simply because they didn't know MBUs existed, while others made arrangements for relatives to care for their babies once born, assuming that their babies would be sent out at birth. We have no way of knowing if any pregnancies have actually been terminated because of this lack of knowledge. Not finding out about existing provision or a facilitated early application can and has had devastating consequences for mothers and their babies – sometimes with long-term consequences. Baldwin is involved in a lived experience led project that will hopefully see posters/leaflets and information about the potential to apply for an MBU space available in arrest suites, police stations, probation offices and courts.

Conclusion

It is alarming that modern-day activists in the field of maternal imprisonment are making similar requests to those made over one hundred years ago. The need for compassion in criminal justice seems at face value to be obvious (Marshall, 2012; Baldwin, 2023), yet '[o]ffending mothers are viewed as undeserving' (O'Malley et al, 2022: 3). The institutionalised thoughtlessness we highlighted with the mothers' experiences herein must be addressed, obviously there are broader structural issues, and although 'structural problems require structural fixes' (Coverdale, 2021: 415), individuals can practice with compassion, kindness and respect.

Baldwin (2017, 2022a) has maintained that many mothers enter prison 'already feeling they have failed as mothers, because of their lived experiences, their life chances and their life choices, which in turn has a significant impact on their self-esteem, maternal identity and maternal emotions' (Baldwin, 2017: 3). Bozkurt (2022: 36) argues that 'the situation is then amplified for minoritised mothers who also have to contend with experiences of racism and discrimination while imprisoned'. Bozkurt (2022) argues that minoritised women in prison can fall into a 'blind spot' in both conventional thinking and in criminal justice related scholarly work and practice, arguing that as a result they and their needs are 'frequently overlooked' and 'misrepresented' (Bozkurt, 2022: 14). Bozkurt argues that for minoritised women's needs to be fully accounted for and factored into any positive change going forwards, then on top of the recommendations already heard, there must be a genuine exploration and understanding of minoritised women's experiences of social and criminal justice and how that intersects with women's experiences of the CJS. Bozkurt also argues that 'it is also essential to consider culture in context, where the racial element would not be a factor, but other forms of oppression such as culture and religion may be evident' (Bozkurt, 2022: 196). Trauma-informed practice must consider maternal trauma, alongside cultural 'shame and honour', and appreciate the intersectionality with other traumas. We absolutely need the CJS to be more trauma-informed, but more than that we also need to ensure that the CJS does not cause additional harm and additional trauma to people who come into contact with its services (Baldwin, 2023).

In our respective research we found that not only was pregnant and new mothers' physical health sometimes compromised by lack of care and a failure to meet women's basic needs, but mothers' mental health suffered too (see also Dolan et al, 2019). Not least because of the shame previously mentioned, but also because of the challenges around accessing support before, during and after prison. Across England, there are now specialist perinatal mental health services across all areas where women can be supported through perinatal mental health difficulties, including dedicated MBUs where both mum and baby can stay during acute episodes of mental illness. However, the picture remains more complicated for women in prison during the perinatal period. Women who find themselves in prison are often the most vulnerable on many levels. The prevalence of mental illness, substance misuse and complex trauma is high and yet, as Vanessa Garrity, National Head of Mental Health, Health in Justice, Practice Plus Group, tells us, "it is not unusual for women not to be able to access community perinatal mental health services as well as alternatives to custody". We share Vanessa's view that the development and improvement of mental health facilities for perinatal mothers in and after prison is vital if we are to avoid further tragedies and a continuation of health inequality.

While there are specifics in both Ms A's and Louise births that were outside of the ordinary, which to some extent made the circumstances of their births unpredictable, one thing that is absolutely a certainty for all pregnant women is that they *will* give birth (unless of course the pregnancy is terminated or miscarried). Thus, there is *always* an element of predictability that should be factored into the care and responses to imprisoned pregnant mothers and indeed women more generally. As we have illustrated in the voices of mothers in this book, women's lives before prison can be chaotic, and affected by mental ill-health, substances, abuse, surveillance and neglect. Therefore, as was the case with Louise (Ms B), not all mothers will be aware they are or could be pregnant. Women whose lives have been controlled or abused by others may find it difficult to trust professionals. Women whose babies have previously been removed from their care will often be even more reluctant to engage with all professionals, even midwives – who they may perceive as all being part of the 'system' that can take their babies. As highlighted in *Mothering Justice* (Baldwin, 2015), key to working with mothers, especially mothers who have lived the life that mothers have described herein, is to create a space of 'emotional safety' which will enable women to reach 'reach the point where they are able to engage' (Baldwin, 2015: 34). Baldwin argues in *Mothering Justice* that the 'very fact of being associated with criminal justice and related agencies as a mother service user leaves women vulnerable to feeling stigma (and the emotional consequences of stigma)' (Baldwin, 2015: 30). For many such mothers and mothers to be, it is not only the fear of judgement in relation to their lived experiences, lifestyle and parenting skills, but additionally the fear of consequences, that may prevent mothers from trusting, or seeking advice, guidance and support. Understanding, acknowledging and appreciating maternal related emotions, trauma and role is key if professionals wish to break down the barriers that stop women engaging (Baldwin, 2015).

While we advocate for reducing women's imprisonment and ending imprisonment for pregnant women, we acknowledge that, for some, prison can be a safer environment during pregnancy, and a prison MBU can provide better support than their pre-prison experiences. However, relying on prison as a safer space raises concerns about the community's shortcomings in providing adequate support. There is a need to improve community-based services for criminalised and vulnerable women, requiring commitment and adequate resources for social work, mental health, addiction services, housing and childcare. Addressing the root causes of challenges, inequality and discrimination faced by women entering prison is essential to break cycles of harm. To achieve positive outcomes in criminal justice, a commitment to social justice is crucial. We support the previous recommendations mentioned in this book and would like to reiterate and add recommendations of our own.

1. We would wish for the stated pursuit of fewer women, to include mothers, pregnant and new mothers, in custody.
2. Increased use of diversion from custody and out of court disposals.
3. Increased funding and a reignited commitment to invest in gendered community-based resources for vulnerable and criminalised women.
4. Gendered sentencing guidelines, with the added requirement (as opposed to a guideline) to avoid sentencing pregnant or new mothers to custody unless in the most extreme of circumstances.
5. Increased funding and commitment for community-based MBUs modelled on resources like Jasmine Mother's Recovery[17] and Hope Street.[18,19]
6. Additional guidelines around recall and remand for pregnant and new mothers.
7. Training for staff on pregnancy, maternal trauma, and new motherhood and motherhood generally for all prison staff.
8. Ensure all community- and hospital-based midwives have training concerning vulnerable and criminalised pregnant women and new motherhood.
9. Embed criminal justice midwifery training into the midwifery qualification training.
10. Embed criminal justice/maternal trauma training into all social work, probation officer and prison officer training.
11. Roll out of the 'pregnancy wing' across the whole of the female estate.
12. Roll out of the birth of ROTL scheme from HMP Peterborough to the whole estate.

13. Actively increase and monitor positive outcomes for MBU applications.
14. Ensure midwifery is reflected in the make-up of the prisons inspectorate.
15. Roll out the good practice currently being utilised to ensure consistency (for example, HMP Low Newton).
16. Increase the number of social workers based in prisons, develop criminal justice social teams and roles.
17. Ensure maternal trauma and racial trauma are understood and accounted for in trauma-informed practice and approaches.
18. Probation supervision must actively factor in motherhood, maternal trauma and pregnancy as a place to interrupt cycles and recognise opportunity.
19. Women with lived experience must be involved in all developments in policy and practice through consultation, development and delivery.
20. Measures must be put in place to ensure consistency across the estate in terms of 'rules' (for example, restraints being removed at hospital).
21. The development of the Motherhood Charter should be supported and maintained, and the Birth Charter revisited and implemented consistently.

We firmly believe that progress in all of the recommended areas would significantly improve the understanding, care and outcomes for pregnant and new mothers. Improvement in social justice, early intervention and a trauma-informed CJS is vital if we are to deliver more fair, intelligent, compassionate and importantly effective criminal justice (Bradley, 2021; Baldwin, 2023). Moreover, trauma-informed approaches with criminalised women must also recognise that 'effective interventions with criminalised women requires both the avoidance of re-traumatization and the presence of respectful and supportive interventions to enable and facilitate women to repair and rebuild their lives' (Baldwin, 2023: 29). Bradley

(2021: 255) calls for the 'Working with Trauma Quality Mark' to be introduced into HMPPS as a 'quality assurance model in order to develop trauma practice, while providing a mechanism to demonstrate and celebrate aspects of good practice across HMPS'. We echo her recommendation and are pleased to see this developing.

It is clear that the Ministry of Justice has demonstrated a willingness to review and improve policy and practice in relation to pregnancy and imprisonment, which makes it all the more anomalous that it was recently announced that there will be 500 more prison spaces for women. This will undoubtedly result in an increase in the number of women imprisoned, and we can only assume this will mean more pregnant women will be imprisoned, meaning many more babies will start their lives in a prison. We strongly feel that a far better illustration of the Ministry of Justice's commitment to positive change would be to support and direct the judiciary in making sure that sending a pregnant women to prison is avoided at all costs, and by the active pursuit and funding of community-based alternatives. The organisation Birth Companions is running a joint campaign with Women in Prison and Level Up, which seeks to end the imprisonment of pregnant women. This campaign has attracted national attention and has secured over 20,000 signatures at the time of going to press, indicating that there is recognition that things must change. We actively support the call for the government to introduce a statutory duty for courts to consider the health of pregnant women and the best interests of children in sentencing decisions, and furthermore to explore all possible alternatives to custodial sentences as a priority. Fundamentally, it must be the case that whatever improvements can and should be made for the care and support of pregnant and new mothers in prison, the preferred option, and ultimate goal, will remain far fewer pregnant women, new mothers and their babies entering the prison space in the first instance.

We would like to end this book with a final contribution by Louise Powell.

Poem for my daughter

Brooke

Having you, I didn't have a clue
This must be happening to someone else
I was scared shocked,
In awe

As soon as I saw you I was mesmerised,
Your beautiful face, your tiny hands, your tiny feet
You were perfect
I was in awe of you

You are with me in the morning, my first thought and
my last at night
Every minute of every day
You are everything, you are everywhere
I'm in awe of you

I'm trying to live my life for you
Fighting for justice as I go
Without you I am broken, crushed
I'm in awe of you

I'd have been the best mum, given you the best life
I'm still a mum, your mum
I'd have loved you unconditionally
I'd have been in awe of you

Brooke-Leigh Powell I will love you until my last breath

Love from, your mum xx

Louise Powell

Notes

one

1   Louise Powell gave birth to her stillborn daughter, Brooke-Leigh, in a toilet at HMP Styal in June 2020. A full investigation was carried out by the PPO (2022).

2   Birth Companions is a women's charity dedicated to tackling inequalities and disadvantage during pregnancy, birth and early motherhood. It was founded in 1996 to support pregnant women and new mothers in Holloway Prison. https://www.birthcompanions.org.uk/pages/8-our-work

3   JHRC (2019) *The Right to Family Life: Children whose Mothers are in Prison* (report and link to televised committee hearing). https://parliament live.tv/event/index/61fd9da1-cf05-4c3a-bd0c-8071e0a52342 https://publications.parliament.uk/pa/jt201719/jtselect/jtrights/1610/report-files/161009.html

4   Women in Prison is a national charity that delivers support for women affected by the CJS in prisons, in the community and through its Women's Centres. https://womeninprison.org.uk/about/our-mission

5   Review of operational policy on pregnancy, mother and baby units and maternal separation' published in July 2022. https://assets.publishing.service.gov.uk/government/uploads/system/uploads/attachment_data/file/905559/summary-report-of-review-of-policy-on-mbu.pdf

6   Prisoners' advice leaflet on guidance for applying for an MBU space. http://www.prisonersadvice.org.uk/wp-content/uploads/2018/06/Mother-and-Baby-Units-Self-Help-Toolkit-June-2018-1.pdf

7   JHRC (2019) *The Right to Family Life: Children whose Mothers are in Prison* (report and link to televised committee hearing). https://parliam entlive.tv/event/index/61fd9da1-cf05-4c3a-bd0c-8071e0a52342 https://publications.parliament.uk/pa/jt201719/jtselect/jtrights/1610/report-files/161009.htm

[8] Assessment, Care in Custody and Teamwork (ACCT) is a document and practice designed to support someone in prison who is at risk of self-harm or suicide. Its primary purpose is to keep people safe.

[9] Davies et al (2022). https://www.nuffieldtrust.org.uk/research/inequality-on-the-inside-using-hospital-data-to-understand-the-key-health-care-issues-for-women-in-prison

[10] *Guardian* report into the story. https://www.theguardian.com/society/2021/sep/22/damning-report-published-into-death-of-baby-born-to-teenager-in-prison-cell

[11] Delayed chorionic villous maturation (DVM) is a type of placental disease that restricts oxygen to the baby and can result in stillbirth. DVM can be due to genetic factors, maternal disease (such as gestational diabetes) or drug or alcohol misuse during pregnancy. It is associated with an increased risk of stillbirth or death in the first few weeks of a baby's life.

[12] Article in the *Guardian*. https://www.theguardian.com/society/2022/jan/11/uk-inmate-gave-birth-to-stillborn-in-prison-toilets-inquiry-finds

[13] Louise Powell was involved in this book, writing her own contribution on page 170, and she requested to relinquish her anonymity for this book, feeling that by doing so her voice and the life of her daughter, Brooke-Leigh Powell, are more openly acknowledged, respected and remembered.

[14] Louise and Lucy Baldwin wrote this tribute to Brooke together, hosted by Russell Webster. https://www.russellwebster.com/a-baby-never-forgotten-a-tribute-to-Brooke-leigh-powell/

two

[1] Jasmine project is a community-based residential unit which can be used an alternative to custody, permitting mothers and children to reside together while the mothers receive targeted multi-agency and specialist support. Children are cared by their mothers with the support of relevant professionals where required. https://trevi.org.uk/services/jasmine-mothers-recovery/

[2] https://www.gov.uk/government/publications/pregnancy-mbus-and-maternal-separation-in-womens-prisons-policy-framework

[3] See note 2 for Chapter 1.

[4] Lockdown means when prisoners are confined to their cells and unable to leave, usually to maintain security or when an emergency has happened.

[5] Abbott's latest research project exploring the forced separation of mothers from their babies during their prison term. www.lostmothers.org

three

[1] Mary Elwood is a pseudonym chosen by 'Mary'.

[2] Women in Prison (2017) *The Corston Report: Ten Years On*. https://women inprison.org.uk/news/corston-10

[3] The Prison Reform Trust states that on 7 January 2022 there were 3,186 women in prison in England and Wales. In the year to June 2021, 4,787 women entered prison, either on remand or to serve a sentence (PRT, 2022).

[4] More than 17,500 children were estimated to be separated from their mothers by imprisonment in 2020. Information on the caring responsibilities of women in prison and children living in the community is not recorded centrally. The government has stated it is considering how to monitor and publish this information. 15 babies were held in prison in a mother and baby unit (MBU) in March 2021. 31 babies were born to women held in prison in the year to March 2021.

[5] The Bangkok Rules on Women Offenders and Prisoners. https://cdn.penal reform.org/wp-content/uploads/2013/07/PRI-Short-Guide-Bangkok-Rules-2013-Web-Final.pdf

four

[1] The Lammy Review (2017). https://www.womeninprison.org.uk/research/reports.php?s=2017-04-21-double-disadvantage

[2] Several positive changes and additional guidance came about following the investigations into the deaths of Baby A and Baby B.

[3] Prison canteen is like the in-house shop where the prisoner (if they have banked funds or a prison wage) can order items such as vapes, biscuits, toiletries, stationery, snacks, crisps, drinks and more.

[4] The mucus plug is a thick piece of mucus that blocks the opening of the cervix during pregnancy. It forms a seal to prevent bacteria and infection from getting into the uterus and reaching the baby. Think of it as a barrier between the vagina and the baby, the mucus plug is often lost as an early sign of impending labour.

[5] All officer/staff names have been changed to preserve confidentiality.

[6] The process of robustly searching a room for contraband, often by a designated prison search team, and most often leaving the room/cell in a state of disarray.

five

[1] Supervised regular contacts organised by social services and usually in a contact centre, with a plan to move gradually to more frequent and unsupervised contacts as part of the process of a gradual full reunification.

[2] Rt Hon Robert Buckland, 31 March 2020. https://www.gov.uk/government/news/pregnant-prisoners-to-be-temporarily-released-from-custody#:~:text=31%20March%202020-,Pregnant%20women%20in%20custody%20who%20do%20not%20pose%20a%20high,be%20released%20with%20their%20children

[3] Drugs.

[4] At the time of wring Ms Powell has an open legal case against the Ministry of Justice and the healthcare provider in the prison (Spectrum).

[5] Following the operational review, mothers are now afforded the same legal rights to maternity leave as women 'outside'. It was not the case when Kady had her baby.

[6] 'A window of opportunity: Understanding the needs and experiences of pregnant women and new mothers in contact with the criminal justice system in the community in England' (2021). https://hubble-live-assets.s3.amazonaws.com/birth-companions/file_asset/file/15/A_window_of_opportunity_Clinks_and_Birth_Companions_FINAL_2021.pdf

six

[1] For more information on Birth Companions' influence in the CJS, see 'This is what change looks like'. https://www.birthcompanions.org.uk/resources/this-is-what-change-looks-like

[2] Review of Operational Policy on Pregnancy, Mother and Baby Units and Maternal Separation (2020). https://assets.publishing.service.gov.uk/government/uploads/system/uploads/attachment_data/file/905559/summary-report-of-review-of-policy-on-mbu.pdf

[3] Birth Companions. https://www.birthcompanions.org.uk/

seven

[1] Review of Operational Policy on Pregnancy, Mother and Baby Units and Maternal Separation. https://assets.publishing.service.gov.uk/government/uploads/system/uploads/attachment_data/file/905559/summary-report-of-review-of-policy-on-mbu.pdf

[2] https://www.welevelup.org/about-us/

[3] The Female Offender Strategy Delivery Plan, 2022–25, published January 2023. https://assets.publishing.service.gov.uk/government/uploads/system/uploads/attachment_data/file/1132790/female-offender-strategy-delivery-plan-2022-25.pdf

[4] Justice services in Wales are delivered by a range of local, regional and national agencies working together. While the UK government retains responsibility for justice and policing, most services related to the wellbeing and resilience of women in Wales have been devolved to the

Welsh government. The complexity of the landscape in Wales means that justice in Wales is delivered as a partnership between devolved and non-devolved organisations.

[5] The custody threshold is contained in s.230 Sentencing Act 2020 which provides that the court must not pass a custodial sentence unless it is of the opinion that the offence, or the combination of the offence and one or more offences associated with it, was so serious that neither a fine alone nor a community sentence can be justified for the offence.

[6] This is not an exhaustive list of positive changes in prisons. All of the prisons in the female estate have made positive changes to a greater or lesser degree since the aforementioned operational review.

[7] https://www.hsj.co.uk/patient-safety-awards/hsj-patient-safety-awards-2018-maternity-and-midwifery-services/7022744.article

[8] Baldwin was commissioned by Sodexo, via Ms Stevens, Women's Policy Lead, to explore and evaluate the current care and consideration of mothers at HMP Peterborough. This included pregnant and new mothers on the MBU.

[9] See note 12 for Chapter 1.

[10] PAUSE work to improve the lives of women who have had – or are at risk of having – more than one child removed from their care, and the services and systems that affect them aiming to support women who experience the removal of children into care are given the best possible support, so that it never happens more than once. https://www.pause.org.uk/about-us/

[11] Guidance for working with women offenders in custody and the community.

[12] Women's Policy Framework (2021). https://assets.publishing.service.gov.uk/government/uploads/system/uploads/attachment_data/file/996349/womens-pf.pdf

[13] The Female Offender Strategy Delivery Plan, 2022–25, published January 2023. https://assets.publishing.service.gov.uk/government/uploads/system/uploads/attachment_data/file/1132790/female-offender-strategy-delivery-plan-2022-25.pdf

[14] Summary of the positive impact of their 2016 Birth Charter. https://hubble-live-assets.s3.amazonaws.com/birth-companions/file_asset/file/683/The_impact_of_Birth_Companions_Birth_Charter_-_online_PDF.pdf

[15] Hibiscus. https://hibiscusinitiatives.org.uk/services/where-we-work/

[16] https://www.welevelup.org/active-campaigns/pregancy-in-prison/#:~:text=After%20months%20of%20research%20with,11%2C000%20people%20signed%20it

[17] Jasmine takes referrals from across the UK and can accommodate up to ten women and their children at any time. https://trevi.org.uk/services/jasmine-mothers-recovery/

[18] Hope Street will pilot a new approach to working with justice-involved women. https://onesmallthing.org.uk/hopestreet

[19] Jasmine Mother's Recovery, Hope Street and Phoenix Futures are community-based alternatives to prison for vulnerable pregnant women in the CJS. They are non-punitive and non-judgemental – and they work.

References

Abbott, L. (2015) A pregnant pause: Expecting in the prison estate. In Baldwin, L. (ed) *Mothering Justice: Working with Mothers in Criminal and Social Justice Settings*. Sherfield on Loddon: Waterside Press, pp 185–211.

Abbott, L. (2018) *The Incarcerated Pregnancy: An Ethnographic Study of Perinatal Women in English Prisons*. Doctoral thesis, University of Hertfordshire.

Abbott, L. (2023) Pregnancy and new motherhood in prison during the COVID-19 pandemic. In Booth, N., Masson, I. and Baldwin, L. (eds) *Experiences of Punishment, Abuse and Justice by Women and Families*. Bristol: Bristol University Press.

Abbott, L. and Tammam, J. (2019) Pregnant women's opinions of the food provided in prison. *Journal of Human Nutrition and Dietetics*, 32(S1), 15–31. https://doi.org/10.1111/jhn.12627

Abbott, L. and Lockwood, K. (2020) Negotiating pregnancy, new motherhood and imprisonment. In *Mothering from the Inside*. Cambridge: Emerald Publishing Limited, pp 49–66.

Abbott, L., Scott, T., Thomas, H. and Weston, K. (2020) Pregnancy and childbirth in English prisons: Institutional ignominy and the pains of imprisonment. *Sociology of Health and Illness*, 42(3), 660–675.

Abbott, L., Scott, T. and Thomas, H. (2023a) Compulsory separation of women prisoners from their babies following childbirth: Uncertainty, loss and disenfranchised grief. *Sociology of Health & Illness*, 45(5), 971–988. https://doi.org/10.1111/1467-9566.13423

Abbott, L., Scott, T. and Thomas, H. (2023b) Experiences of midwifery care in English prisons: Findings from ethnographic research. *Birth*, 50(1), 244–251.

Arendell, T. (2000) Conceiving and investigating motherhood: The decade's scholarship. *Journal of Marriage and Family*, 62(4), 1192–1207.

Arshad, F., Haith-Cooper, M. and Palloti, P. (2018) The experiences of pregnant migrant women in detention: A qualitative study. *British Journal of Midwifery*, 26(9), 591–596.

Bachman, R., Kerrison, E.M., Paternoster, R., Smith, L. and O'Connell, D. (2016) The complex relationship between motherhood and desistance. *Women and Criminal Justice*, 26(3), 212–231.

Baldwin, L. (ed) (2015) *Mothering Justice: Working with Mothers in Criminal and Social Justice Setting*. Sherfield on Loddon: Waterside Press.

Baldwin, L. (2017) Tainted love: The impact of prison on maternal identity. *Prison Service Journal*, 223, 28–34. https://www.crim eandjustice.org.uk/sites/crimeandjustice.org.uk/files/PSJ%20 233%20September%202017.pdf

Baldwin, L. (2018) Motherhood disrupted: Reflections of post-prison mothers in maternal geographies. *Emotion Space and Society*, 26, 49–56. https://www.sciencedirect.com/science/article/abs/pii/ S1755458616300500?via%3Dihub

Baldwin, L. (2019) Motherhood judged, social exclusion mothers and prison. In Byvelds, C. and Jackson, H. (eds) *Motherhood and Social Exclusion*. Toronto: Demeter Press, pp 129–144.

Baldwin, L. (2020a) 'A life sentence': The long-term impact of maternal imprisonment. In Lockwood, K. (ed) *Mothering and Imprisonment*. Emerald Publishing, pp 85–101.

Baldwin, L. (2020b) Why has another baby died in prison? *Russell Webster*, 24 June. https://www.russellwebster.com/pri son-baby-death/

Baldwin, L. (2021a) Motherhood challenged: Exploring the persisting impact of maternal imprisonment on maternal identity and role. Summary of doctoral thesis, De Montfort University. https://dora.dmu.ac.uk/bitstream/handle/2086/21372/Execut ive%20Summary%20PhD%20LBaldwin%20PDF.pdf?sequence= 3&isAllowed=y

Baldwin, L. (2021b) Executive summary, motherhood challenged: Exploring the persisting impact of maternal imprisonment on maternal identity and role. Summary of doctoral thesis, De Montfort University. January 2021.

Baldwin, L. (2022a) *Mothers in and after Prison*. Sherfield on Loddon: Waterside Press.

Baldwin, L. (2022b) Missed and lost opportunities: Recognising maternal trauma in probation supervision. *Probation Quarterly*, 23, 16–20. https://doi.org/10.54006/TDRY6231

Baldwin, L. (2022c) 'Mothering from the inside'; Evaluation of first 12 month project for Sodexo (HMP Peterborough). Unpublished.

Baldwin, L. (ed) (2023) *Gendered Justice: Trauma Informed Working with Criminalised Women*. Sherfield on Loddon: Waterside Press.

Baldwin, L. and Epstein, R. (2017) *Short but not Sweet: A Study Exploring the Impact of Short Custodial Sentences on Mothers and their Children*. Coventry: De Montfort University and Oakdale Trust. https://www.nicco.org.uk/userfiles/downloads/5bc450 12612b4-short-but-not-sweet.pdf

Baldwin, L. and Abbott, L. (2020) Why do we still imprison pregnant women? *Russell Webster*, 1 July. https://www.russellwebster.com/pregnant-prisoners/

Baldwin, L. and Abbott, L. (2021) Incarcerated motherhood: Reflecting on 100 years of imprisoning mothers. *Prison Service Journal*, 257, 29–38.

Baldwin, A., Sobolewska, A. and Capper, T. (2020) Pregnant in prison: An integrative literature review. *Women and Birth*, 33(1), 41–50.

Baldwin L., Elwood, M. and Brown, C. (2022a) Criminal mothers: The persisting pains of maternal imprisonment. In Grace, S., O'Neill, M., Walker, T., King, H., Baldwin, L., Jobe, O., Lynch, F., Measham, K., O'Brien, K. and Seaman, V (eds) *Criminal Women: Gender Matters*. Bristol: Policy Press, pp 107–131.

Baldwin, L., Parent, K., Wray, B. and Mulcahy. J (2022b) 'Out of sight out of mind': Arguing the case for social workers in women's prisons. *Prison Service Journal*, 263, 48–54.

Baradon, T., Fonagy, P., Bland, K., Lénárd, K. and Sleed, M. (2008) New beginnings: An experience-based programme addressing the attachment relationship between mothers and their babies in prisons. *Journal of Child Psychotherapy*, 34(2), 240–258.

Barnes, C. (2015) Damned if you do, damned if you don't: Frontline social worker perspective. In Baldwin, L. (ed) *Mothering Justice: Working with Mothers in Criminal and Social Justice Settings*. Sherfield on Loddon: Waterside Press, pp 65–89.

Barton, A. (2000) 'Wayward girls and wicked women': Two centuries of 'semi-penal' control. *Liverpool Law Review*, 22(2–3), 157–171.

Bennett, R. (2017) *Identifying & Advocating for Women's Health: The Duchess of Bedford's 1919 Committee of Enquiry into Medical Care in Holloway Prison*. https://warwick.ac.uk/fac/arts/history/chm/research/current/prisoners/outputs/duchess_of_bedford.pdf

Birth Companions (2019) *Birth Charter Toolkit*. https://www.birthcompanions.org.uk/resources/135-the-birth-charter-toolkit

Birth Companions (2020) *Your Inside Guide to Pregnancy, Birth and Motherhood in Prison*. https://hubble-live-assets.s3.amazonaws.com/birth-companions/attachment/file/228/Your_inside_guide_to_pregnancy__birth_and_motherhood_in_prison.pdf

Birth Companions (2021) *A Window of Opportunity: Understanding the Needs and Experiences of Pregnant Women and New Mothers in Contact with the Criminal Justice System in the Community in England*. https://hubble-live-assets.s3.amazonaws.com/birth-companions/redactor2_assets/files/315/A_window_of_opportunity_Clinks_and_Birth_Companions_FINAL_2021.pdf

Booth, N. (2020) *Maternal Imprisonment and Family Life: From the Caregiver's Perspective*. Bristol: Policy Press.

Bosworth, M. (2000) Conforming femininity: A history of gender, power and imprisonment. *Theoretical Criminology*, 4(3), 265–284.

Bozkurt, S. (2022) *Behind Bars: Exploring the Prison and Post Release Experiences of Minoritised Mothers*. Doctoral thesis, University of Westminster. https://westminsterresearch.westminster.ac.uk/item/vz803/behind-bars-exploring-the-prison-and-post-release-experiences-of-minoritised-mothers

Bozkurt, S. and Thomas, M. (2023 'Racism is very much there': Validating racial trauma in the context of criminal justice. In Baldwin, L. (ed) *Gendered Justice: Trauma Informed Working with Criminalised Women*. Sherfield on Loddon: Waterside Press, pp 99–117.

Bradley, A. (2021) Viewing Her Majesty's Prison Service through a trauma-informed lens. *Prison Service Journal*, 255, 4–11.

Broadhurst, K. and Mason, C. (2020) Child removal as the gateway to further adversity: Birth mother accounts of the immediate and enduring collateral consequences of child removal. *Qualitative Social Work*, 19(1), 15–37. https://doi.org/10.1177/147332501 9893412

Brown, M. and Bloom, B. (2009) Re-entry and renegotiating motherhood: Maternal identity and success on parole. *Crime and Delinquency*, 55(2), 313–336.

Bryman, A. and Burgess R.G (2002) *Analysing Qualitative Data*. London: Routledge, pp 1–17.

Cahalin, K., Callender, M., Lugli, V. and Weston, C. (2021) Perinatal women's experiences of access to expertise, information and appropriate medical attention in prison. *Prison Service Journal*, 257, 12–21.

Carlen, P. (1985) Law, psychiatry and women's imprisonment: A sociological view. *The British Journal of Psychiatry*, 146(6), 618–621.

Carlen, P. and Worrall, A. (2004) *Analysing Women's Imprisonment*. Cullompton: Willan Publishing.

Chigwada-Bailey, R. (2003) *Black Women's Experiences of Criminal Justice: Race, Gender and Class: A Discourse on Disadvantage*. Sherfield on Loddon: Waterside Press.

Clarke, B. and Chadwick, K. (2018) From troubled women to failing institutions: The necessary narrative shift for the decarceration of women post Corston. In Moore, L., Scraton, P. and Wahidin, A. (eds) *Women's Imprisonment and the Case for Abolition: Critical Reflections of Corston Ten Years On*. London: Routledge, pp 51–71.

Codd, H. (2008) *In the Shadow of Prison: Families, Imprisonment and Criminal Justice*. Devon and Portland: Willan Publishing.

Corston, J. (2007) *The Corston Report: A Report by Baroness Jean Corston of a Review of Women with Particular Vulnerabilities in the Criminal Justice System*. London: Home Office.

Coverdale, H.B. (2021) Caring and the prison in philosophy, policy and practice: Under lock and key. *Journal of Applied Philosophy*, 38(3), 415–430. https://onlinelibrary.wiley.com/doi/pdfdirect/10.1111/japp.12415

Crawley, E. (2005) Institutional thoughtlessness in prisons and its impacts on the day-to-day prison lives of elderly men. *Journal of Contemporary Criminal Justice*, 21(4), 350–363.

Crewe, B., Hulley, S. and Wright, S. (2017) The gendered pains of life imprisonment. *British Journal of Criminology*, 57(6), 1359–1378.

Davies, M., Keeble, E. and Hutchings, R. (2021) Injustice? Towards a better understanding of health care access challenges for prisoners. *Nuffield Trust*. https://www.nuffieldtrust.org.uk/files/2021-10/1634637809_nuffield-trust-prisoner-health-2021-final.pdf

Davies, M., Keeble, E., Hutchings, R. and the Nuffield Trust (2001). *Injustice: Towards a Better Understanding of Health Care Challenges for Prisoners*. www.nuffieldtrust.org.uk/sites/default/files/2021-10/1634637809_nuffield-trust-prisoner-health-2021-final.pdf

Dolan, R. (2018) *Pregnant Women in Prison: Mental Health, Admission to Prison Mother and Baby Units and Initial Outcomes for Mother and Child*. Doctoral thesis, University of Manchester. https://www.research.manchester.ac.uk/portal/files/184636089/FULL_TEXT.PDF

Dolan, R., Shaw, J. and Hann, M. (2019) Pregnancy in prison, mother and baby unit admission and impacts on perinatal depression and 'quality of life'. *The Journal of Forensic Psychiatry & Psychology*, 30(4), 551–569.

Eaton, M. (1993) *Women After Prison*. Buckingham: Open University Press.

Egeland, B. and Farber, E.A. (1984) Infant-mother attachment: Factors related to its development and changes over time. *Child Development*, 55(3), 753–771.

Epstein, R. (2011) Mothers in prison: The rights of the child: Rona Epstein looks at whether the courts take into account the rights of children when imprisoning mothers. *Criminal Justice Matters*, 86(1), 12–13.

Epstein, R. (2021) Sentencing mothers: The rights of the child. In Donson, F. and Parkes, A. (eds) *Parental Imprisonment and Children's Rights*. London: Routledge, pp 168–186.

Epstein, R., Brown, G. and de Frutos, M. (2022) Why are pregnant women in prison? Report. Coventry University. https://www.coventry.ac.uk/globalassets/media/global/08-new-research-section/cawr/pregnant-women-in-prison-a4-final-report.pdf

Farmer, M. (2019) *The Importance of Strengthening Female Offenders' Family and Other Relationships to Prevent Reoffending and Reduce Intergenerational Crime*. London: Ministry of Justice.

Galloway, S., Haynes, A. and Cuthbert, C. (2014) *All Babies Count – An Unfair Sentence: Spotlight on the Criminal Justice System*. London: NSPCC.

Garcia-Hallett, J. (2019) Maternal identities and narratives of motherhood: A qualitative exploration of women's pathways into and out of offending. *Feminist Criminology*, 14(2), 214–240.

Garland, D. (1985) *Punishment and Welfare: A History of Penal Strategies*. Aldershot: Gower.

Gelsthorpe, L. and Morris, A. (eds) (2002) *Feminist Perspectives in Criminology*. Buckingham: Open University Press.

Ghate, D. and Hazel, N. (2002) *Parenting in Poor Environments: Stress, Support and Coping*. London: Jessica Kingsley Publishers.

Goffman, E. (1963) *Stigma: Notes on the Management of Spoiled Identity*. New Jersey: Penguin.

Grace, S., O'Neill, M., Walker, T., King, H., Baldwin, L., Jobe, A., Lynch, O., Measham, F., O'Brien, K. and Seaman, S. (2022) *Criminal Women*. Bristol: Bristol University Press.

Hackett, L. (2015) Working with women and mothers experiencing mental distress. In Baldwin, L. (ed) *Mothering Justice: Working with Mothers in Criminal and Social Justice Settings*. Sherfield on Loddon: Waterside Press, pp 43–65.

Harding, N. (2020) Co-constructing feminist research: Ensuring meaningful participation while researching the experiences of criminalised women. *Methodological Innovations*, 13(2). https://doi.org/10.1177/2059799120925262

Health and Social Care Committee (2018) *The State of Health and Care in English Prisons*. London: UK Parliament. https://publications.parliament.uk/pa/cm201719/cmselect/cmhealth/963/96302.htm

Independent Monitoring Boards (2021) *Annual Report of the Independent Monitoring Board at HMP/YOI Bronzefield for Reporting Year 1 August 2020–31 July 2021*. https://s3-eu-west-2.amazonaws.com/imb-prod-storage-1ocod6bqky0vo/uploads/2021/11/Bronzefield-2020-21-annual-report-for-circulation.pdf

Johnstone, H. (2019) Imprisoned mothers in Victorian England, 1853–1900: Motherhood, identity and the convict prison. *Criminology & Criminal Justice*, 19(2), 215–231.

Leverentz, A. (2014) *The Ex-Prisoner's Dilemma: How Women Negotiate Competing Narratives of Re-entry and Desistance*. New York: Rutgers University Press.

Liss, M., Schiffrin, H. and Rizzo, K. (2013) Maternal guilt and shame: The role of self-discrepancy and fear of negative evaluation. *Psychological Science*, 5. https://scholar.umw.edu/psychological_science/5

Marshall, C.D. (2012) *Compassionate Justice: An Interdisciplinary Dialogue with Two Gospel Parables on Law, Crime, and Restorative Justice* (Vol 15). New York: Wipf and Stock Publishers.

Martin, K. and Powell, C. (2021) Mother-infant separations in prison: Why does context matter? In Masson, I. and Booth, N. (eds) *Handbook of Women's Experiences of Criminal Justice*. Abingdon: Routledge, pp 388–401.

Masson, I. (2019) *Incarcerating Motherhood: The Enduring Harms of First Short Periods of Imprisonment on Mothers*. Oxon: Routledge.

Mayhew, H. and Binny, J. (2011) *The Criminal Prisons of London: And Scenes of Prison Life*. Cambridge: Cambridge University Press.

MBRRACE-UK (2021) *Saving Lives, Improving Mothers' Care: Lessons Learned to Inform Maternity Care from the UK and Ireland Confidential Enquiries into Maternal Deaths and Morbidity 2017–19.* https://www.npeu.ox.ac.uk/assets/downloads/mbrrace-uk/reports/maternal-report-2021/MBRRACE-UK_Maternal_Report_2021_-_FINAL_-_WEB_VERSION.pdf

Ministry of Justice (2018) *Female Offender Strategy.* London: Ministry of Justice.

Ministry of Justice (2020) *Summary Report of the Review of PSI 49/2014 and Operational Policy on Pregnancy and Women Separated from Children under 2 in Prison.* 31 July. Open Government Licence. https://assets.publishing.service.gov.uk/government/uploads/system/uploads/attachment_data/file/905559/summary-report-of-review-of-policy-on-mbu.pdf

Ministry of Justice (2023) *Female Offender Strategy Delivery Plan 2022–25.* https://assets.publishing.service.gov.uk/government/uploads/system/uploads/attachment_data/file/1132790/female-offender-strategy-delivery-plan-2022-25.pdf

Ministry of Justice and HMPPS (2021) *Pregnancy, Mother and Baby Units (MBUs), and Maternal Separation from Children up to the Age of Two in Women's Prisons.* https://assets.publishing.service.gov.uk/government/uploads/system/uploads/attachment_data/file/1023428/mbu-pf.pdf

Ministry of Justice Statistical Release (2021) 3 of 31 births. *HMPPS Annual Digest, April 2020 to March 2021.* www.gov.uk

Minson, S. (2020) *Maternal Sentencing and the Rights of the Child.* Cham: Palgrave Macmillan.

Minson, S. (2021) The impact of COVID-19 prison lockdowns on children with a parent in prison. Report. https://www.law.ox.ac.uk/content/impact-covid-19-and prison-lockdown-children-imprisoned-parent-uk

Morley, C. and Rushton, C. (2023) Gendering justice: Adopting a whole-systems approach and why a women's specialist team model makes sense. In Baldwin, L. (ed) *Gendered Justice: Trauma Informed Working with Criminalised Women.* Sherfield on Loddon: Waterside Press, pp 37–61.

Morriss, L. (2018) Haunted futures: The stigma of being a mother living apart from her child(ren) as a result of state-ordered court removal. *The Sociological Review*, 66(4), 816–831.

Mulligan, C. (2019) Staying together: Mothers and babies in prison. *British Journal of Midwifery*, 27(7), 436–441. https://www.british journalofmidwifery.com/content/literature-review/staying-toget her-mothers-and-babies-in-prison/

National Prison Healthcare Board (2019) *Principle of Equivalence of Care for Prison Healthcare in England*. https://assets.publishing.service. gov.uk/government/uploads/system/uploads/attachment_data/ file/837882/NPHB_Equivalence_of_Care_principle.pdf

Nursing and Midwifery Order, 45 Statutory (2001) Department of Health. http://www.legislation.gov.uk/uksi/2002/253/pdfs/ uksi_20020253_en.pdf

Observer (2021) Jailed women in UK five times more likely to suffer stillbirths data shows. *Observer*, 5 December. https://www.the guardian.com/society/2021/dec/05/jailed-women-in-uk-five-times-more-likely-to-suffer-stillbirths-data-shows

O'Keefe, C. and Dixon, L. (2015) *Enhancing Care for Childbearing Women and their Babies in Prison*. http://www.birthcompanions. org.uk/media/Public/Resources/Extpublications/FINAL_MB U_r eport_8th_December_2016.pdf

O'Malley, S. (2018) *The Experience of Imprisonment for Incarcerated Mothers and their Children in Ireland*. Doctoral thesis, NUI Galway.

O'Malley, S. and Devaney, C. (2016) Supporting incarcerated mothers in Ireland with their familial relationships: A case for the revival of the social work role. *Probation Journal*, 63(3), 293–309.

O'Malley, S. and Baldwin, L. (2019) Mothering interrupted: Mother-child separation via incarceration in England and Ireland. In Beyer, C. and Robertson, A. (eds) *Mothers Without Their Children*. Toronto: Demeter Press.

O'Malley, S., Baldwin, L. and Abbott, L. (2021) Starting life in prison: Reflections of the UK and Irish contexts of pregnant and new mothers in prison, through a children's rights lens. In Donson, F. and Parks, A. (eds) *Presenting a Children's Rights Approach to Parental Imprisonment*. London: Routledge, pp 87–113.

O'Malley, S., Devaney, C. and Millar, M. (2022) Incarcerated mothers' experience of adversity heard using participatory mixed-method research. *Probation Journal*, 1–19. https://doi.org/10.1177/02645505221143335

Opsal, T.D. (2011) Women disrupting a marginalized identity: Subverting the parolee identity through narrative. *Journal of Contemporary Ethnography*, 40(2), 135–167.

Powell, C., Marzano, L. and Ciclitira, K. (2017) Mother–infant separations in prison: A systematic attachment-focused policy review. *The Journal of Forensic Psychiatry & Psychology*, 28(2), 274–289.

Pitman, J., Hull, J. and Crest (2021) *Counting the Cost of Maternal Imprisonment: Insights Report*. London: Crest Advisory. https://www.crestadvisory.com/post/report-counting-the-cost-of-maternal-imprisonment

PPO (Prisons and Probation Ombudsman) (2015) *Independent Investigation into the Death of Ms Michelle Barnes a Prisoner at HMP Low Newton on 16 December 2015*. https://www.ppo.gov.uk/app/uploads/2017/04/L229-15-Death-of-Ms-Michelle-Barnes-Low-Newton-16-12-2015-SID-31-40.pdf

PPO (Prisons and Probation Ombudsman) (2021) *Independent Investigation into the Death of Baby A at HMP Bronzefield on 27 September 2019*. https://s3-eu-west-2.amazonaws.com/ppo-prod-storage-1g9rkhjhkjmgw/uploads/2021/09/F4055-19-Death-of-Baby-A-Bronzefield-26-09-2019-NC-Under-18-0.pdf

PPO (Prisons and Probation Ombudsman) (2022) *Independent Investigation into the Death of Baby B at HMP&YOI Styal on 18 June 2020*. https://s3-eu-west-2.amazonaws.com/ppo-prod-storage-1g9rkhjhkjmgw/uploads/2022/01/F4376-20-Death-of-Baby-B-Styal-18-06-2020-NC-Under-18-0.pdf

PRT (Prison Reform Trust) (2022) *Bromley Briefings Prison Factfile Winter 2022*. https://prisonreformtrust.org.uk/publication/bromley-briefings-prison-factfile-winter-2022/

Raikes, B. and Lockwood, K. (2011) 'Mothering from the inside': A small scale evaluation of Acorn House, an overnight child contact facility at HMP Askham Grange. *Prison Service Journal*, 194, 19–26.

Redshaw, M. and Martin, C. (2013) Babies, 'bonding' and ideas about parental 'attachment'. *Journal of Reproductive and Infant Psychology*, 31(3), 219–221.

Rees, A., Waits, C. and Bezeczky, Z. (2023) *'Together a Chance': Evaluation of the Social Worker for Mothers in Prison Pilot Project, 2021–2023 Second Interim Report*. Cardiff: Cascade and Pact. https://www.prisonadvice.org.uk/Handlers/Download. ashx?IDMF=cf29a773-603f-492a-b1c7-8877d11ef16d

Renzetti, C.M. (2013) *Feminist Criminology*. Abingdon: Routledge.

Sharpe, G., Gelsthorpe, L. and Worrall, A. (2009) Looking for trouble: A recent history of girls, young women and youth justice. *Youth Justice*, 9(3), 209–223.

Sikand, M. (2015) *Lost Spaces: Is the Current Procedure for Women Prisoners to Gain a Place in a Prison Mother and Baby Unit Fair and Accessible?* London: The Griffins Society.

Smoyer, A.B. and Lopes, G. (2017) Hungry on the inside: Prison food as concrete and symbolic punishment in a women's prison. *Punishment & Society*, 19(2), 240–255.

Stewart, P.W. (2015) A psychodynamic understanding of mothers and babies in prison. In Baldwin, L. (ed) *Mothering Justice: Working with Mothers in Criminal and Social Justice Settings*. Sherfield on Loddon: Waterside Press, pp 167–185.

Sykes, G.M. (2007 [1958]) *The Society of Captives: A Study of a Maximum-Security Prison*. Princeton: Princeton University Press.

Thomas, M. (2023) *'Just because I've gone to prison, my mum hat doesn't switch off': An Analysis of Black Mothers' Narratives of Imprisonment and Life after Release*. Unpublished thesis, Cardiff University.

Thornburg, K., Patterson, A. and Zhang, L. (2014) Programming and the barker hypothesis. In Zhang, L. and Longo, L.D. (eds) *Stress and Developmental Programming of Health and Disease: Beyond Phenomenology*. Nova Science Publishers, Inc.

Torchalla, I., Linden, I.A., Strehlau, V., Neilson, E.K. and Krausz, M. (2014) 'Like a lots happened with my whole childhood': Violence, trauma, and addiction in pregnant and postpartum women from Vancouver's Downtown Eastside. *Harm Reduction Journal*, 11(1), 1–10.

Trowler, I. (2022) Applications to mother and baby units in prison: How decisions are made and the role of social work: A case review of social work decision making (2017–2021), 24 November. Gov.Uk. https://assets.publishing.service.gov.uk/government/uploads/system/uploads/attachment_data/file/1119733/Applications_to_mother_and_baby_units_in_prison_-_how_decisions_are_made_and_the_role_of_social_work.pdf

Warr, J. (2016) The deprivation of certitude, legitimacy and hope: Foreign national prisoners and the pains of imprisonment. *Criminology & Criminal Justice*, 16(3), 301–318.

Wismont, J.M. (2000) The lived pregnancy experience of women in prison. *Journal of Midwifery and Women's Health*, 45(4), 292–300.

Zedner, L. (1991) Women, crime and penal responses: A historical account. *Crime and Justice*, 14, 307–362.

Index

Page numbers in *italic* type refer to figures. As 'pregnant women in prison' is the main topic of the book, index entries under this heading have been kept to a minimum and readers are advised to seek more specific topics.